At times, we all need to be inspire[illegible] e do, and to live with a larger visior [illegible] Jones delivers that insp[illegible] n a punch in his new book, *The Left-Handed Warrior*. With no excuses and no holds barred, he pushes each of us to believe in ourselves and to live a life of *doing* rather than just dreaming. I encourage you to devour this transforming book. Absorb these teachings in your core as you live large, with the wind in your face and with nothing held back.

—Dr. Dave Martin
"Your Success Coach" and author of *Twelve Traits of the Greats*

Pastor Jamie Jones has written an absolute instruction manual on moving forward in faith. Read this book and prepare to be inspired not to settle. When you put these time-honored principles to work, get ready to shatter the walls of containment in your life!

—Jim Raley
Lead pastor at Calvary Christian Center, Ormond Beach, FL, and author of *Hell's Spells: How to Identify, Take Captive, and Dispel the Weapons of Darkness* and *Dream Killers: Igniting the Passion to Overcome Your Obstacles and Mistakes*

Looking for perfection is the mother of all procrastination! How easy it is to be overwhelmed by the "strength" of what is a life-challenging obstacle in front of us while focusing on the perceived "deficiencies" in our own ability. Within the pages of his book, *The Left-Handed Warrior*, my friend, Pastor Jamie Jones, will give you courage to engage your moment of opportunity and discover the life you were born to live!

—Bishop Tony Miller
Pastor of The Gate Church, Oklahoma City, OK; bishop of Destiny Network International; and author

We are so quick to give God reasons as to why He can't use us. *The Left-Handed Warrior* will not only challenge that thinking, but will empower you to go after your dreams despite what you may consider faults. Pastor Jamie Jones is able to beautifully convey a powerful message that will make you get off your couch and chase the impossible.

—Kristen Alvarez
Founder and CEO of lovedearly.org

It is a joy to recommend the excellent book, *The Left-Handed Warrior,* by Pastor Jamie Jones. It is a study of the heroic and delivering act by Ehud recorded in the third chapter of Judges. Pastor Jones makes it clear that God can, and will, use anyone who recognizes a challenge, believes God, answers the call, and acts swiftly and decisively. This manuscript will benefit everyone from experienced leaders to rookies in their first assignment. Its inspiration and instruction invites us to righteous action and shows us how to be successful. Read it. It will teach you how to be a great warrior—even if you aren't left-handed!

—Reverend Terry Raburn
Superintendent Peninsular Florida District Council of the Assemblies of God

Great accomplishments start with believing in yourself. The first step is knowing who you are and understanding that as a child of God, you are positioned for greatness. I love stories and books like this one that encourage and reinforce the truth that our Father has created a masterpiece in each of us. *The Left-Handed Warrior* is a remarkable book of inspiration and hope for living with boldness and confidence.

—Christine Martin
Author of *Recharged*

When I heard Jamie preach to a standing-room-only crowd in Addis Ababa, Ethiopia, I knew that he was special. His new and incredible book called *The Left-Handed Warrior* puts you on the front seat of exciting reading. Once you begin, it will be almost impossible to put the book down. Jamie is an incredibly motivating speaker and writer, who has the passion necessary to help you tell the world, "Jesus is the Answer!"

—Sam Johnson
Executive director and founder of Priority One

From the very first page of this book, the mind of a man is engaged with a flair for a supernatural reckless abandon. Jamie Jones is not writing a book for the mere spiritual success of the believer, but for the world domination in the Holy Spirit that can arise when the principles and practical measures of this book are engaged. Don't wait: *Read* and *live abundantly*!

—Allen Griffin
Evangelist and author of *Undefeated: Ditch the Poor Choices and Live Free*

I have known Jamie Jones ministry for years! His new book, *The Left-Handed Warrior,* is a challenge to us all—young and old. It's a healthy reminder that God never wants to stop using us, but we still have to be the ones who get out of the boat. Game changer for sure!

—Trent Cory
Lead pastor of Hope City United, Albany, GA and international recording artist

Looking for the courage to do what you know God is leading you into, but afraid to take the leap of faith? This page turner will revive your belief that God can use you to do anything He directs. Stop standing on the outside looking in: *"Pull the trigger"* and discover what God may be calling you to do.

—Todd M. Diedrich
Author of Daily Dose: *A 90-Day Remedy to Encountering a Fresh View of God*

Countless books have been written that encourage, give hope and map out strategies to overcome. Pastor Jamie accomplishes this and then some in *The Left-Handed Warrior*. He challenges us to draw and wield the sword of the Spirit and charge into battle with full assurance that the God of miracles is present today, has clearly spoken, and will pave the way to victorious living.

—Tim Hamilton
Owner of Harleysdirect.com

Pastor Jamie Jones has already earned our attention by his dynamic preaching and ability to challenge and motivate us to step out from the mundane of mediocrity to the realization of our potential in Christ. *The Left-Handed Warrior* takes our gifts, talents, and what we might consider hindrances in our life and catapults them to achieve the unimaginable, the miraculous, and the impossible. This book will revolutionize your relationship with Christ.

—Susan Pippin
Pastor, Assemblies of God Women's Ministries Representative and author of *Susan's Coffee Break Devotional*

Many people are living out their day-to-day lives with frustrated purposes: daydreaming during the time to act and sleeping during the moments to dream. Because of this, I am thankful pastor and author Jamie Jones has released a life-changing book that will awaken our society from the slumber of complacency. This astounding message ushers the courage for one to take action, pull up the anchor of our excuses and hoist the sails of belief once again. *The Left-Handed Warrior* is encouraging, challenging and practical: all of which thrust the reader to act upon the assignment God has given them to fulfill. I highly recommend this book. I know you won't be able to put it down.

—Timothy McCain
Opening Eyes Ministries

Pastor Jamie Jones has written a must-read challenge to everyone who might be hesitant to "step out of the boat" and take a shot at walking on the water. God has created us to be adventurers: people who discover His marvelous creations that help build our faith. This practical manual is a guide full of applied faith experiences that can help us make a choice or a decision. It needs be in your briefcase or on your digital device as a quick faith-building resource that will assist in enlarging your faith and result in living an exciting, fulfilling life.

—Larry E. Hazelbaker, Ph.D
Professor of psychology, Southeastern University, Lakeland, FL

In every generation God raises up bold witnesses who bring to the surface the dire need for a spiritual shift within the church, leading to transformational change for those who are living under debilitating weakness and fear. With the entrance of *The Left-Handed Warrior*, we are alerted to the faithful plan God has for each of us, a motivating truth of which Pastor Jamie Jones is such a witness. This passionate and piercing book will renew your spirit and reveal your absolute purpose to soar high and successfully conquer the impossible. As the church, we must never ignore our clear call to move beyond the ordinary into the extraordinary. Be sure to read this book. Be sure to live this book.

—Mark Nelson
Samaritan's Purse

From the time we are just children we have all been challenged by the dreams we have. How to move from it just being a dream, to making the dream a reality, is a process that often eludes us. Pastor Jamie Jones in this gripping and intriguing story, gives us some powerful and insightful truths, through the life of Ehud that will help us move toward the realization of the dream God has placed in our heart.

—Roy Pippin
Pastor of Highest Praise Church, Tarpon Springs, FL

Many times when our lives are at a standstill when it seems that nothing is happening, we stand back and keep waiting on God. But many times God is looking at His people and saying, "I am waiting on you!" Pastor Jamie has written a book that encourages us to have a faith that is full of action. I believe that your faith will be both challenged and equipped to go to a whole new level as you read. Let the words on these pages inspire you to believe in a God who is an Expert at doing the impossible!

—Wayne Northup
Lead pastor, Saints Community Church, Metairie, LA

In *The Left-Handed Warrior*, Jamie Jones gives practical insight into how God can use an ordinary person, like you and me, to do extraordinary things. Jamie shows us how God takes our weaknesses and uses them to make His name great. I love the encouragement and vision in this new book! If you have ever felt like you were not equipped to accomplish amazing exploits, get ready, because this book will prepare you to take new and exciting risks for the kingdom of God.

—Reverend Darin Poli
Executive pastor, River Valley Church, Minnesota

The Left-Handed Warrior

Rise up and be the one nobody saw coming

Jamie Jones

5 Fold Media
Visit us at www.5foldmedia.com

The Left-Handed Warrior: Rise Up and Be the One Nobody Saw Coming

Published by 5 Fold Media, LLC
www.5foldmedia.com

Front cover design by Matthew Armon.

ISBN: 978-1-942056-59-1

Library of Congress Control Number: 2017961277

Printed in the USA.

Dedication

This writing is dedicated to the bravest woman I know. She also happens to be the woman to whom I've given my heart. My wife, Michelle Jones, has looked adversity right in the eye and caused it to cower in the shadow of her faith. She has truly taken what was designed to be her demise, and turned it into an earth-shaking testimony. She isn't just a survivor, she is an overcomer and a warrior. Thank you for your support during this writing, but more importantly, thank you for your example of faith. I love you more than words can say.

Acknowledgments

I would like to thank all who contributed by praying and supporting me in making this writing possible.

To my three kids, Kristen, James, and Joshua, you make me more proud than you'll ever know.

To my parents and grandparents, whose stories have been major contributors to this writing.

Sherry Dalto, thank you for dealing with all my commas and other mistakes.

To my staff, thank you for enduring my focused endeavor.

Trinity Church, thank you for being so supportive.

Jesus, thank You for saving me and allowing me the privilege to preach Your Word.

Contents

Foreword

Foreword

In his powerful book, *The Left-Handed Warrior*, my dear friend Pastor Jamie Jones has written a masterpiece that will awaken those whom God has appointed for such a time as this! This book takes us on a journey into the life of Ehud, an Old Testament judge who God used to bring a revolution that would lead to eighty years of peace in Israel. Ehud also reminds us that God's greatest warriors are often those who have hidden gifts that the world calls "handicaps." As you read each page you will feel as if Jamie must have been reading your personal story as he was writing, or better yet, maybe God was talking directly to Jamie about *you*! I warn you to not read this book unless you are ready to make your *dash* (the line on your tombstone between your birth and death) actually count! In fact, while you are reading this book, remember this verse: "Whatever I tell you in the dark, speak in the light; and what you hear in the ear, preach on the housetops" (Matthew 10:27).

As I read this book, I knew that it was written by a man who understands the meaning of Proverbs 13:12: "Hope deferred makes the heart sick, but when the desire comes, it is a tree of life." I truly believe that we are now living in an hour when hope must be restored. This book is an antidote for a disease called hopelessness. If you feel like God could never use you, Jamie teaches us in *The Left-Handed Warrior* that God can pull you out of the pit of self-depreciation and call you into a life of victory. This book will minister greatly to you if you fall into one of the following categories:

If you are frustrated, you are a prime candidate to be used of God. After all, frustration and agitation are the mother of intercession. God's will for each of us is to finish the race He has called us to run. This means there are times when God will frustrate you until you realize you were called to be an overcomer. The apostle Paul wrote, "For the creation was subjected to futility, not willingly, but because of Him who subjected it in hope; because the creation itself also will be delivered from the bondage of corruption into the glorious liberty of the children of God" (Romans 8:20-21). In other words, God will frustrate you in the hope of bringing you into a life of freedom.

If you feel forgotten, Jamie teaches that God has been looking for you. You will learn that we are now living in an hour where it is time for those whom have seemed to be hidden and forgotten to arise and lead. I have often said that the greater the anointing, the greater the isolation. God has always had the key to the lost-and-found closet.

If you are ready, it is time to take back your moment. In one moment, God can shift everything. If you will dedicate yourself to pursuing the Lord, preparing for battle, and living purposely past your limitations, then you will step into your destiny. This book will awaken those asleep at the wheel, revive those in need of the *pneuma* (breath) of God, and restore those whom are living in the land of lost dreams. It teaches us that God loves to use those He knows will give all praise back to Him!

From cover to cover, this book is a war cry, declaring, "This is your *now*!" Will you be the spark that ignites a fire in this generation? Only time will tell!

—Pat Schatzline
Evangelist and author, Remnant Ministries International

Introduction

Introduction

Have you ever dreamed of doing incredible things for God; but that dream gets quickly interrupted by self-doubt? I stand behind this statement: "God can use anyone to do anything!" I've seen far too many people who have allowed their perceived weaknesses to sideline them and keep them from pursuing their dreams that seem so far out of reach. God has this incredible ability to take what appears to be our weakness, or even our handicap, and use it to accomplish the impossible.

The story explored in these chapters is about this very thing, and will help you discover what God intended you to be. This story is about an up-and-coming warrior who had no idea how far God was going to take him. His perceived weakness was exactly what God was looking for to do the impossible. My prayer is that you will find something much deeper in these pages than a historical account of a little-known battle. May you find your inner warrior.

My intent in writing *The Left-Handed Warrior* goes beyond telling a story that deserves to be told. This book is written to move you to action. Inside each of us, there is untold potential and possibility. When we allow ourselves to be blinded by our own weakness, it keeps us from achieving God's best. The warrior in this story had some things to overcome, but his willingness, obedience, and availability positioned him to do the unthinkable. This story is bigger than a man on a mission; his obedience led to the freedom of an entire nation.

Don't think of this as a book to "read"; think of it as a book to "do." We all know that God does great things through "other" people, but what about people like you? There's a reason that so much attention has been brought to your weakness. It's because Satan doesn't want you to realize that it can become your greatest asset! Let's move on to action and begin chapter one!

Chapter 1: Secret Agent

Chapter 1: Secret Agent

Beginning in the early 1950s a film series began to make itself known all around the world. It was a movie saga about a British secret service agent. The agent had incredible abilities and a mystery-solving sense of smell that could be paralleled by no one else. He had an assortment of gadgets that would make any tool collector jealous, and he knew exactly how to use each of them at precisely the right moment.

Watching these films, which have been produced and released for decades now, is entertaining and thought-provoking. Although we'd like to believe all of these scenarios are possible, we have to remind ourselves that this is a big screen Hollywood movie production at its best. The little boy still inside me (deep inside me), still wonders... what if? What if it were actually possible to do death-defying stunts, use technological gadgets with pinpoint accuracy, and solve mysteries with wizard-like skill? What if we could be real life undercover agents?

I don't know about taking it to that extreme, but I do know that God has plans for us. He has plans for us that are much bigger than we realize. In fact, I believe His plans for us are so big that even the most notorious secret agent would look inferior in comparison to our incredible potential.

> "For I know the thoughts that I think toward you, says the Lord, thoughts of peace and not of evil, to give you a future and a hope" (Jeremiah 29:11).

Divine Special Intelligence

A secret agent receives special communications and intelligence briefings that give him or her information needed to complete his or her assignment. It would be impossible to expect an agent to be successful if not given enough information to begin his or her work. A good agent is a master at taking small slivers of intelligence and piecing the clues together in order to find the people he is looking for. God has a special briefing protocol with us as well. His special intelligence is delivered directly from the throne and downloaded into our spirits. This is a place of deep consecration and intimacy where God reveals the secrets of heaven to empower the abilities of man.

> "He who dwells in the secret place of the Most High shall abide under the shadow of the Almighty" (Psalm 91:1).

David knew something about the secret place; this was the place in which he learned to run in his time of need. He had lived a very tumultuous life, starting out as a shepherd but quickly being brought into the king's courts after he slayed the famous giant, Goliath. There were quite a few people who had David in their crosshairs, people who were jealous as a result of their own desire for prominence. David found shelter in the presence of God. As a psalmist, he worshiped the Lord out in the fields while watching sheep. It was in this environment that God was creating David to be the man who would eventually lead His nation.

Deep communion with God is not in an undisclosed location; it is a place of open invitation.

The secret place that David found was a place he learned to run to when seeking guidance, and also one in which he could depend in times of desperation. The secret place wasn't a secret hideout that only a few people knew about, but rather a place of communion with God. David cried out to the Lord in desperation and God heard him. In David's secret place, battle plans were created, strategic decisions were made, hope was restored, and major policy changes were formulated.

This place of deep communion with God is not in an undisclosed location; it is a place of open invitation. It is a place that is available to us right now.

> "Let us therefore come boldly to the throne of grace, that we may obtain mercy and find grace to help in time of need" (Hebrews 4:16).

The very throne room of God is always open to us. It is open to come in and hear God's desires and to know His plans for us. Secret agents who are responsible for highly classified information are highly dependent upon good intelligence. A bad lead can take them down a path that can waste precious man-hours. When we trust in the Lord and hear from Him, our intelligence is always solid. God wants you to succeed just as much, if not more, than you want to succeed!

Finding the Secret Place

I remember a time very early in our ministry when we were going through some difficulties. We were in a new church plant which was seeing some success, but was struggling to get up and off the ground. At the time, I was working a part-time overnight job at a grocery store while spending long hours in our new ministry. We had young kids at home and were struggling financially as well as trying to find our place in God's calling. My wife and young family really wanted to be obedient to the Lord, but were going through the same growing pains that many endure when first starting out.

There were times the Enemy really worked on me. At times, I felt like I had missed God's plan by launching out in this new ministry too soon. We had a lot of family talks, stayed supportive of each other, and we prayed together. There were other ministers who were very helpful to me and gave us their advice coming from years of experience, for which I'm eternally grateful. Even with all of this support and extra encouragement, I needed more in order to really sustain my path. The truth is, I really needed to get alone with the Lord for myself and get confirmation from Him as to my call.

It was during this time of discouragement that I entered a season of fasting. One day I was praying in the sanctuary of our rented and refurbished old bank building. I began to cry out to the Lord over our situation, seeking God's guidance as to what He wanted our future to look like. I was willing to comply with whatever the Lord would say, but I needed to hear His voice for myself. What happened next, I'll never forget.

There was a knock at the front door of our facility. My first response was to ignore it, simply because I was deep in prayer. I decided to go and see who was knocking, and to my amazement, it was a pastor friend of mine who I hadn't seen in quite a while. When I opened the door, he said, "The Lord told me to come by and encourage you today." I thought I was going to pass out! There is no way that this was coincidence; this was God sending me someone to help me in my time of need.

The secret place of God is not found in a simple, leisurely, or religious stroll. The secret place of God is found by intense prayer and pressing in to the Lord. God knew exactly what I needed in that moment. That man will never really know how much he helped me, nor the answer to prayer that he became for me. I was fasting at the time, and this pastor told me he wanted to take me to lunch. Well, who am I to argue with God? We had a great time of fellowship, and I walked away strengthened and encouraged by the Lord.

Ehud's Untold Story

In the old secret agent movies, the actors are known for their witty one liners and fast responses. This all looks good on film and makes for a great story, but seldom do we have all the answers we need. Sometimes our lack of answers can breed insecurities that keep us from pursuing everything God has for us. In the secret place, confidence is born because we know God is with us and He will not fail! We're going to take a little journey now: a journey into an historical place in which strength and power were the order of the day. A place where one false move could mean your life; a place where people had to be very careful with the alliances they formed. One false move, one bad relationship, one communication error could cost you your life.

Lack of answers can breed insecurities that keep us from pursuing everything God has for us.

This journey will begin with a story that is somewhat buried in Scripture. I say "buried" because it's not usually given a lot of airtime, and I've spent a lifetime in church but have rarely heard much about it. It is about an Old Testament judge and warrior by the name of Ehud. Ehud may not have a film series named after him or even one that would make an indirect reference to his specific skill set, but he is certainly a man worthy of discussion. He completed an undercover assignment; in fact, it was an assassination operation. This operation would take nerves of steel and a steady hand and, of course, some help from God Himself.

Judges 3 shows us that the people of Israel were under extreme oppression and forced to serve a people stronger than them. This was a painful time in Israel's history and it lasted for eighteen years. Imagine that! Eighteen long years of serving a nation that was idolatrous and ruthless. The people of Moab came to recognize Israel as little more than slaves: people required to pay annual tribute and heavy taxes. The oppression was more than the people could bear, and after eighteen years they finally said enough is enough! They began to cry out to the Lord and He responded.

> "But when the children of Israel cried out to the Lord, the Lord raised up a deliverer for them: Ehud the son of Gera, the Benjamite, a left-handed man" (Judges 3:15).

The people needed more than a revolt; they needed more than a political coup; they needed an absolute revolution. They needed a revolution that would break the back of Moabite bondage and set their people free. They wanted to see their children grow up in a place where they were respected and had hope for a successful future. They wanted a place in which people wouldn't aspire only to be free, but aspire to be great without barriers of bondage and restriction. They needed someone or something that could reverse the process of deepening pain and sorrow. Israel was oppressed both economically and spiritually. The Moabites were known for their idolatry and inhumane worship practices. For this cycle of bondage to end, something had to change. Something big, something out of the ordinary, something nobody would ever see coming. Who or what could possibly do this? Were they doomed for an endless cycle of generational bondage? They were a country in need, but in need of what? Although they didn't realize exactly what they needed, God did; and He gave them their secret agent.

The Assassination

By all accounts Ehud was a fairly average guy. No stellar résumé, no lengthy letters of recommendation, just a left-handed man from the tribe of Benjamin. We do know that he was Israel's second judge, but there were no additional standout details given about him. Out of all the people who could have been chosen, why would God choose Ehud? Why would He choose this particular left-handed judge to carry out an assassination attempt that would change Israel's history?

Ehud's plan was one that proved to be pretty simple and did not involve a large amount of diplomacy or external involvement. No explosive devices, no radar, no satellite spies, no infrared detection devices. Just a man, a sword, a bag of money, and some intense faith. When the tribute to Moab was brought to King Eglon, Ehud asked for a private consultation. After the king agreed, the rest was history.

> "So Ehud came to him (now he was sitting upstairs in his cool private chamber). Then Ehud said, 'I have a message from God for you.' So he arose from his seat.

> Then Ehud reached with his left hand, took the dagger from his right thigh, and thrust it into his belly. Even the hilt went in after the blade, and the fat closed over the blade, for he did not draw the dagger out of his belly; and his entrails came out. Then Ehud went out through the porch and shut the doors of the upper room behind him and locked them" (Judges 3:20-23).

Did you catch that? This man held a private meeting with the king, successfully assassinated him, locked out the guards from entering the room, and snuck out a window, completely undetected! If that's not a secret agent execution, I don't know what is! After his successful operation, Ehud rallied the troops of Israel to attack the people of Moab and they were successful in breaking the stronghold of their oppression.

Who would have thought this could even take place? Would anyone have believed it would be so easy? If it were this simple, why hadn't anyone done this before? I mean, if it were that simple, anyone could have done it, right? Keep in mind, although Ehud was an ordinary person, he served a God who was anything but. Ehud was average, yes, but He was raised up by God for just this moment. There was a unique combination of God's anointing, preparation, opportunity, and availability that took this assassination from a simple idea to a successful completion. Where are the secret agents today? Where are those who realize that they are inadequate in themselves, but with the hand of God upon their life they can do the unthinkable?

What if God has plans for me that are so far beyond the scope of my imagination, that if I actually knew what they were, I would shake with fear?

Did this covert operation require Ehud? Were there other men like Ehud who God was drawing to complete this task, who due to their fear or unavailability, didn't respond as Ehud did? Perhaps there were heroes waiting in the wings who just didn't fulfill their purpose. This is the thing that I am the most concerned about in my own life. What if God has plans for me that are so far beyond the scope of my imagination, that if I actually knew what they were, I would shake with fear? This book is for the secret agents out there, those who know that God has plans for them and are willing to listen and pursue His will.

Dream Big

I don't believe Ehud ever imagined himself as a secret agent, one who would pull off one of the most successful assassinations ever recorded in history. I believe he saw himself simply as a vessel. A vessel that God could use. This caused him to be more than just a judge, but a hero. Ehud's ability was never highlighted, but his obedience sure was. As you wake up each day, know that God has greater plans for you today than the day before. Scripture reminds us of just how much God wants to do in us.

> "Those who do wickedly against the covenant he shall corrupt with flattery; but the people who know their God shall be strong, and carry out great exploits" (Daniel 11:32).

There is a big difference between covenant "breakers" and covenant "makers." Throughout history we've seen people who wasted their opportunities. People like Adam and Eve, who gave heed to temptation and squandered their incredible potential. People like Esau, who, for a pot of stew, sold his birthright and lived to regret that decision for the rest of his life. Anyone can break an agreement, but only the strong can see it through to the end. God says, "The people who know their God shall be strong, and carry out *great exploits*." Doing great exploits is a natural outflow of really truly "knowing" our God. If we really know who He is, we can't help but operate in the realm of the supernatural. We can't help but have extraordinary faith! We can't help but take a stand against unrighteousness and ungodliness. We can't help but pursue our fullest potential! We can't help but think it is perfectly plausible to sneak in and take out an ungodly and oppressive king… all by ourselves!

> If we really know who He is, we can't help but operate in the realm of the supernatural.

As a little boy, I dreamed of being a secret agent, a spy who was both fearless and unstoppable. For some reason, I never became that spy. But I did realize that the dream inside of me was in a raw form. God never intended that I run covert missions for the U.S. government, (at least not up to this point in my life, anyway), but He did intend that I be that fearless and unstoppable force I dreamed about. That force wouldn't be shown in physical strength or combat skills in the natural, but in the spiritual realm instead. Each day we limit ourselves by our own capacity to dream. I hope this writing will encourage you to dream again. When I say dream, I mean really dream: big, crazy, unbelievable dreams. I mean the kind of dream that when fulfilled, everyone will know that had to be God!

Ehud had to dream of what it would be like to walk into the chambers of King Eglon and carry out a successful assassination. How many times did that play over and over in his mind until he finally actually lived it out? He dreamed it so many times that when he did it, he probably felt like he had done it before. When Ehud drove that dagger deep into the belly of the wicked king, it was more than success; it was the fulfillment of a dream. This dream would be one that would free the Hebrews from oppressive bondage and religious restriction. This dream would carry Ehud into the memoirs of history as one of the greatest warriors of all time.

Take the Risk

Many times we are hindered by our own insecurities. As a child I dreamed of standing in front of a group of people and preaching the gospel. In fact, I routinely gathered all of my stuffed animals on the bed in my room to create a makeshift church. I stood at the end of my bed and preached my heart out to that wild conglomeration of "church folk." I led worship, I received an offering (we never collected much money though), and I gave a powerful altar call. Crazy blue-haired puppets, long-necked giraffes, and movie characters of all sorts got saved by the droves. Man, I'm telling you, we had some serious church; complete with aisle runners and exuberant worshipers! I didn't realize it at the time, but God was stirring the fire of the gift He was imparting to me even then.

Fast forward through a rough teenage stint, then open rebellion followed by a radical salvation experience, and once again I realized God was working on me. I volunteered in my local church as a youth leader and God began opening the door for me to be involved more heavily. The first time I was asked to preach to a group of teenagers I was scared to death. I was nineteen years old and afraid of public speaking. I paced the floor for hours in my home before agreeing to accept this overwhelming challenge. As I was praying and preparing to speak, God brought something back to my mind. It wasn't my sin as a teenager or even the years I had spent in complete rebellion against God. He reminded me of something He had begun in me many years before that. You guessed it: A child standing at the end of a bed preaching to a bunch of stuffed animals! Was it actually possible that a boy preaching to a thrown together assortment of stuffed animals was actually being trained to do something bigger than he ever dreamed possible? What if I had missed it? What if I was actually supposed to be working in the toy industry and just got my signals crossed? Sometimes you have to step out and trust the Lord.

But what if Ehud really missed it? I mean, what if he had it all wrong and wasn't really supposed to go and attempt this assassination? God, what if what I'm hearing You ask me to do, isn't really You? My question is this: Can you afford to take a chance on being wrong? Better yet, can you afford to take a chance on never knowing because you never tried? The success of a secret agent is built on their willingness to take risks. If there was no risk involved, what excitement would there really be?

If there were no risks then I guess just about anyone could successfully carry out secret missions.

The success of a secret agent is built on their willingness to take risks.

God has not called us to play it safe and have no risk, but rather to have bold faith in Him. When we truly follow Him and trust Him, He is actually the One who assumes all the risk! Yes, it moves us out of our comfort zone and creates some uncertainty, but isn't that what faith is all about?

> "Now faith is the substance of things hoped for, the evidence of things not seen" (Hebrews 11:1).

Coming Out of the Comfort Zone

If Ehud had an absolute guarantee of victory, there would have been no faith required. When he stepped into the king's chambers, you better believe he felt some apprehension and anxiety. The key is this: Anxiety cannot be allowed to dictate our actions. Ehud had some uncertainty: What if he was discovered? What if the king didn't allow the private meeting? What if an eavesdropping guard overheard the stabbing and busted through the doors? What if he chickened out at the last minute? Moving in faith will always come with its own specific set of unique "side effects" and "what if" fears.

If you're waiting to be obedient to God until everything lines up and all your fears are alleviated, guess what? The Devil has been successful in stopping you. Not only did he stop you, but he stopped you before you even started. If Ehud would have allowed his apprehension to keep him from his planned attack, Israel's history would have been forever changed. I'm thankful that there have always been Ehuds, Christian secret agents who are willing to take risks and move forward. I would rather try and fail than never try at all. When we never try, we'll never know what could have been, or better yet, what should have been.

> A dreamer sometimes stands alone, but great men will stand, even if they have to stand by themselves.

I am hoping to appeal to that inner part of you that still has a dream. Sometimes reality has a way of stifling our dreams, and the rigors and routine of life lull us to sleep. It's easy to settle for less; after all, less is not as much work as striving for more! There is a dreamer inside of you, and your faith has the ability to wake him or her up. Ehud couldn't settle for the status quo. I'm sure anyone who heard his plan, though well intentioned, tried to stop him. After all, it would have sounded crazy! But there's a reason he entered into the king's chambers all alone. A dreamer sometimes stands alone, but great men will stand, even if they have to stand by themselves. We are conditioned to see how "other" people do incredible things and how "other" people are extraordinary. What about you? What about the fact that God made a no-name Ehud to be the modern-day equivalent of a heroic secret agent?

Lessons from Failure

When I reluctantly agreed to my first speaking opportunity, I was scared spitless, literally. My mouth was so dry because of anxiety I could hardly open my mouth to speak at all. I tried to keep forcing water down, but all that did was make me have to go to the bathroom! I can still remember the violent butterflies in my stomach that had me precariously positioned somewhere between nausea and absolute terror. The youth pastor gave me a thirty-minute window to share my heart with a group of about fifty unruly teenagers. They were quite the intimidating bunch, let me tell you. I got up and began to speak, but a very strange thing happened. The material I had rehearsed for days on end was strangely dissolving into thin air! In preparation, my thoughts were all over the place, so I began to cut out part after part until I had one streamlined message. I had worked to condense my material to fit within my time frame but because of nervousness I was speaking so fast I sounded like a chipmunk! What I thought I would have to squeeze down to fit into my time constraints took me all of eight minutes. There I was, in front of the church youth group, with an opportunity to speak and nothing left to say! Now I was trying to remember some of the things I cut out so I could add them back in. As hard as I tried to think on my feet, my mind just couldn't recall the information, so I did the next best thing: I went back and reiterated some key points and tried to add a story or two, but guess what? Even with all the stretching, my own nerves would only allow me to speak for a total of eleven minutes. I preached everything I knew and still...only eleven minutes! Man, I was embarrassed and discouraged afterwards.

Had I made a mistake by accepting this opportunity? Was I missing my calling to one day be a preacher? Were those days of "stuffed animal preaching" proving to actually be my nemesis, rather than my preparation? I had some great people like my wife and some of the youth leaders come around me and encourage me when I was finished. I am so glad they did, because I don't know where I would be today had that not happened.

Every secret agent knows that not every assignment ends in success. We read about Ehud's great victory, but I'm sure there were plenty of failures in his past. Do you realize that every time you fail you are learning a valuable lesson that can be learned in no other way? When you make a mistake, it creates a little etch in your mind. That little etch is painful to think about, but it serves as a powerful reminder of some needed adjustments. I would love to tell you that the next time I preached it was a home run. I would love to tell you that, but if I did, it would be a lie! In fact, I preached numerous sermons that were absolute flops before I ever began to have any success in public speaking. Actually, all these years later I still have quite a few flops, but I have reached a degree of confidence in my calling from God.

I would have liked to have been a fly on the wall the day Ehud succeeded in killing the strong-willed, stubborn, and ungodly king of the Moabites. I would have loved to have seen the look on the king's face when he realized that he had been duped. Better yet, I would have loved to have seen Ehud slide out a window with spy-like stealth and run away, realizing he had just done the impossible. I wish I could have seen the look on the people's faces when they realized what had just happened. The moments leading up to and immediately following this assassination will be locked into the history books of heaven for eternity. I could only imagine the feeling of overwhelming success as Ehud breathed a sigh of relief, knowing that God had shown Himself strong yet once again. What growth Ehud's faith must have experienced when all of this was a memory in his mind. Our victories in life become powerful markers to which our future faith is calibrated. I know God will be faithful to me in my future because He has always been faithful to me in my past! Can you imagine speaking with Ehud years after this victory? Can you imagine what it would be like to say to Him: "I don't know if I can do this" or "I don't know if God is able to use me." I believe Ehud would simply sit back, and with sage wisdom, say, "Let me tell you a story…" Man, what a story that would be, coming from his mouth.

Our victories in life become powerful markers to which our future faith is calibrated.

This story is about a man of faith. This is a story about a man with a dream, a belief in his God, and the willingness to see things through to completion. This is a story about a regular guy with regular needs and a normal life. This is a story about a person who is a lot like you and me. Sure, we didn't live in that era of history, and we aren't in bondage to a suppressive and ungodly power. However, we are God's creation, just like Ehud. We are people designed and purposed to do powerful things. God is still looking for faithful people to do things nobody will do and believe for things nobody else will believe for. God is looking for some secret agents. Will you take that challenge?

Chapter 2: The Curse Broken

Chapter 2: The Curse Broken

To really understand the curse that the people of Israel were under, and the full implication of Ehud's incredible victory, you have to dial back in history to about 1900 BC.[1] This story can be found in Genesis, and it involves a man by the name of Lot. Lot was Abram's nephew and an active participant in God's plan for national Israel.

Abram and Lot were both very wealthy men and had many employees, servants, family members, and possessions. They were so wealthy, in fact, that they began to stress the land of its resources.

> "Now the land was not able to support them, that they might dwell together, for their possessions were so great that they could not dwell together" (Genesis 13:6).

As these men continued together as one big happy family, they quickly realized they had to make a change. They could no longer continue together, but had to separate in order to be able to sustain their great companies. Abram was the bigger man, so he decided to give Lot the choice of where he would go and Abram would take the leftovers.

> "So Abram said to Lot, 'Please let there be no strife between you and me, and between my herdsmen and your herdsmen; for we are brethren. Is not the whole land before you? Please separate from me. If you take the left,

1. "Time Line Survey of Bible Events," Time Line Survey of Bible Events, accessed October 04, 2017, http://www.bibletruths.net/archives/btar199.htm.

> then I will go to the right; or, if you go to the right, then I will go to the left'" (Genesis 13:8-9).

Making the Right Decision

Now Lot had a decision to make, and this decision would have enormous consequences for years to come. This wasn't simply picking a house to buy; this was choosing a land to settle the entire extended family. This choice would have an effect on him now and also for the generations of the future. Lot's choice would be indicative of his character and reveal the true inner motives of Abram's nephew. Imagine, having the ability to look up and choose wherever you wanted to go and wherever you wanted to settle permanently. Abram was in covenant with God to choose his dwelling place and had the ability to give land to whomever he chose. Lot, as a family member of Abram's, was able to enjoy some of the favor given to him and experience God's blessing as his own.

With the pressure of generational implications; Lot made his choice. I wonder what pressures weighed upon him as he made this decision. Was his wife involved? Were his kids pulling at his shirttails, saying, "Daddy let's go here" or "Daddy let's go there"? I don't really know, but I would have to assume there was some level of "political" process going on.

The hard decision more often than not is actually the right decision.

Like most decisions we make, there is a right choice and then there is a convenient and easier choice. The two sometimes overlap, but my experience has been that they usually do not. The hard decision more often than not is actually the right decision. As we look at the story of Ehud, he clearly had an incredibly difficult decision to make. The easier choice would have been to allow things to continue the way they had been going. The difficult choice was to take a stand and do something about the oppression he and his people were experiencing.

There have been decisions in my life that were incredibly difficult to make, but after praying and getting confirmation from God, those decisions turned out to be correct. I had been a successful youth pastor for several years, and my family and I were very comfortable. Things were going well for us and for the church we were involved in. I loved my church, I loved the people, and I loved my pastor and his family. We were cared for and growing under their leadership. I had no idea what was coming around the corner, but God sure did. The Lord began to speak to me about starting a new church. This church wouldn't be one that would be in competition with where I was in ministry; it would be about thirty miles away. At first glance, this was a crazy idea. Why would I leave this place of comfort, success, and stability to launch out on my own with no promise of success?

The walk of faith is a journey into the unknown.

As my wife and I began to pray about this, we realized that this was more than just the wild idea of a twenty-four-year-old wide-eyed preacher. We really felt like this was God. There were many people around us who didn't understand our decision. Many thought we were crazy and even prophesied failure over the church-to-be. This decision was hard; it would have been easier to just stay put. My pastor understood where we were coming from and was a strong voice of support in our decision. He even volunteered to help back us financially! The easy decision would have been incorrect: Stay and continue to enjoy the comfort of job security and good pay. That sounds right. We knew there was a decision we needed to make. This decision was hard and, looking at it from a common-sense approach, it didn't make sense. The walk of faith is a journey into the unknown.

After much prayer, soliciting counsel, and soliciting finances, we launched out on this new endeavor. God favored us incredibly, and in spite of our lack of experience, blessed us greatly. It wasn't always easy.

In fact there were many obstacles, but God did miracle after miracle for us in that season of our lives. We were in that area for five years until God moved us, but I'm happy to report that as of this writing, that church continues to do well and is a strong ministry today. It all started with a decision, a decision to be obedient and trust God. Much of life comes down to the decisions we make. Though seldom easy, God gives us the peace to make the right decisions. In the story of Lot and Abram, Lot was faced with an all-important, potentially life-changing decision. After some deliberation, it all came down to one choice.

The Implications of Lot's Choice

Lot made that final decision. His decision would take him far from his Uncle Abram into a place he knew little about. The place he chose was a place that had a far-reaching reputation. It wasn't a place known for its incredible devotion to God, or even a place known to be a haven to raise young families in peace and security. The place that Lot chose would prove to be a place of pain and regret that impacted his entire life.

> And Lot lifted his eyes and saw all the plain of Jordan, that it was well watered everywhere (before the Lord destroyed Sodom and Gomorrah) like the garden of the Lord, like the land of Egypt as you go toward Zoar. Then Lot chose for himself all the plain of Jordan, and Lot journeyed east. And they separated from each other (Genesis 13:10-11).

The place he chose was a place that was well watered and fruitful. This place, because of its natural fertility, was a draw for local commerce. With all the business and foreign travelers coming to make money, there was also a draw that was much bigger. The draw was sin! The hunger for money and the lust of the flesh was on the open market. Prostitution, perversion, and ungodliness of all kinds were on open display. This was the region in which the infamous Sodom and Gomorrah were found.

We can't be sure what motivated Lot to make this decision. From an economic perspective, I'm sure it made a lot of sense, but from a spiritual perspective, it was big trouble waiting to happen. Lot may have had some outside influence in his decision, or he may have just looked at its obvious economic promise. Whatever the reason, Lot made the easy call. The easy call was the plain of Jordan, but this call would cost him dearly.

The story continues. For a time, Lot and his family seemed to do pretty well. The kids grew up and they came to know this region as home. However, the sin of the land increased more and more over time until God decided to put a stop to it. The land of Sodom and Gomorrah were so heavily involved in sexual sin and idolatry that God chose to destroy the cities. These are the cities in which Lot and his family had settled.

Before Sodom and Gomorrah were destroyed, Lot was given opportunity to remove his family. As bad as his original choice had been, we see God's powerful grace working in his life.

> "So it came to pass, when they had brought them outside, that he said, 'Escape for your life! Do not look behind you nor stay anywhere in the plain. Escape to the mountains, lest you be destroyed'" (Genesis 19:17).

Lot's original decision was selfish and without any support from God. I believe he made this choice in an effort to take the best land for himself and satisfy the fleshly desires of his family. Now that seed of selfishness was beginning to bring forth fruit. The seed of selfishness will bear the fruit of pain and discomfort for us and those associated with us.

"Remember Lot's Wife"

Lot was running for his life to escape God's wrath being poured out in this region. The land was cursed because of sin. Although Lot was a blessed man, he aligned himself with a curse. His decision caused him and his family joy in the beginning, but unspeakable sorrow in the end. The command was clear: "Do not look behind you nor stay anywhere in the plain." Lot had to leave immediately and was forbidden to even look back. Lot's wife fell into sin by being disobedient. She looked back and as a result, was turned into a pillar of salt. The words of Jesus give us a little better picture of what actually happened:

> "'In that day, he who is on the housetop, and his goods are in the house, let him not come down to take them away. And likewise the one who is in the field, let him not turn back. Remember Lot's wife. Whoever seeks to save his life will lose it, and whoever loses his life will preserve it'" (Luke 17:31-33).

Jesus is using Lot's wife as an illustration to show us the dangers of looking longingly at things we should clearly separate from. Regardless of how attractive a decision may look initially, a bad decision bears bad consequences. Lot is displaced from his home, removed from where his kids had grown up. Lot went from the lap of luxury into hiding in a cave. His wife was gone and his family was fearful about their future. Perilous times bring about harsh circumstances and sometimes even more painful decisions.

Regardless of how attractive a decision may look initially, a bad decision bears bad consequences.

Sins of the Daughters

The daughters of Lot were hurt and confused. Their mother was dead and their father was clearly without a strong plan for the future. Out of desperation the girls made a decision. This decision would also cause the family great pain, pain that would last for many generations. Out of their fear of what the future held for them, these girls came up with a plan to preserve the lineage of their father.

> "Then Lot went up out of Zoar and dwelt in the mountains, and his two daughters were with him; for he was afraid

> to dwell in Zoar. And he and his two daughters dwelt in a cave. Now the firstborn said to the younger, 'Our father is old, and there is no man on the earth to come in to us as is the custom of all the earth. Come, let us make our father drink wine, and we will lie with him, that we may preserve the lineage of our father.' So they made their father drink wine that night. And the firstborn went in and lay with her father, and he did not know when she lay down or when she arose."
>
> "It happened on the next day that the firstborn said to the younger, 'Indeed I lay with my father last night; let us make him drink wine tonight also, and you go in and lie with him, that we may preserve the lineage of our father.' Then they made their father drink wine that night also. And the younger arose and lay with him, and he did not know when she lay down or when she arose."
>
> "Thus both the daughters of Lot were with child by their father. The firstborn bore a son and called his name Moab; he is the father of the Moabites to this day. And the younger, she also bore a son and called his name Ben-Ammi; he is the father of the people of Ammon to this day" (Genesis 19:30-38).

These girls got their father drunk, and then lay with him so they could be impregnated by him. This incestuous relationship would be a thorn in the side of Israel for generations to come. Lot's bad decision set up the events that eventually led to Lot's daughters equally bad decisions, which eventually led to a painful history for the people of Israel. The name of Lot's son by his oldest daughter was Moab. In the Hebrew language, the name Moab means, "son of his father."[2] Could you imagine going around with a name that marks you as a child of incest for your entire life? Everyone knew that Moab was illegitimate. I imagine this young man had some serious personal issues with rejection and insecurity.

2. James Strong, Strong's exhaustive concordance of the Bible (New York: Abingdon Press, 1890).

This young man's name was Moab. Did you catch that name? He would be the father of the Moabites, the ones who would have an ongoing conflict with the children of Abraham for generation after generation. Now, move forward in history to the time of the judges and guess who Israel is still dealing with? That's right, the descendants of that child, born in sin, the Moabite people. Like a bad cold, this Moabite curse was hanging on and had never been resolved. This conflict would last from the time of Abraham ~ 1900 B.C. until the time of the story of Ehud ~ 1400 B.C.[3] At this time, the Moabites had Israel enslaved and were demanding heavy annual tribute and taxes from them. Lot's decision had created an ongoing problem in Israel's history that lasted 500 years! When you are tempted to believe that one small decision may not have lasting effects, remember this story!

The Curse of Moab

During the period of the judges, when Ehud was in leadership, Moab was a very complex problem. It wasn't just about a people who God had raised up during this time to oppress Israel because of their unfaithfulness. It was about an ongoing conflict, a curse that had begun 500 years earlier with an incestuous relationship. The curse began with selfish motivation and now continued throughout the years with bad blood and the desire for revenge. Ehud's assassination of Eglon, the king of Moab, was more than a political move. Ehud represented a people crying out for freedom from the curse of bondage they had experienced for eighteen long years.

It is interesting though, that God is the One who brought Moab back to the surface. I'm sure many people thought that Moab was a buried issue that was no longer a concern. Especially now! Israel itself is in great sin; they are living lives of complete abandonment to the things of God. God realizes that drastic action is necessary to get His people back on track. The old unresolved sin of Moab comes back to the surface. This wasn't a simple skirmish between two families; this was something that God Himself began.

---

3. "Time Line Survey of Bible Events," Time Line Survey of Bible Events, accessed October 04, 2017, http://www.bibletruths.net/archives/btar199.htm.

> "And the children of Israel again did evil in the sight of the Lord. So the Lord strengthened Eglon king of Moab against Israel, because they had done evil in the sight of the Lord. Then he gathered to himself the people of Ammon and Amalek, went and defeated Israel, and took possession of the City of Palms" (Judges 3:12-13).

In order to correct Israel, God chose the very thing that lay beneath the surface of Israel's history. This was the one thing that brought shame to the people as they discussed their history. This was the one story that parents were reluctant to share with their kids because of its graphic nature and the shame associated with it. In order for the people to have spiritual awakening and freedom from their enemies, they would have to defeat the descendants of this original sin.

Sometimes the key to freedom in the present is to seek out freedom from the past.

Going Back to Move Forward

It is interesting how God will sometimes bring us back to areas of our life that need to be healed. There are many times that people will subconsciously suppress thoughts or memories of things they've done in their past. Sometimes the past is too painful to actively remember. Sometimes the key to freedom in the present is to seek out freedom from the past. The powerful thing about Jesus though, is that the grace of God is retroactive. That means that when He forgives us of our sins, it's not the sin of our current state, but the sin of all we've ever done in our past.

> "'Come now, and let us reason together,' says the Lord, 'though your sins are like scarlet, they shall be as white as snow; though they are red like crimson, they shall be as wool'" (Isaiah 1:18).

The Israelites were waiting for someone to step in and break the Moabite curse. Somebody had to say, "Enough is enough!" and do something about it. For them, it came by way of the second judge of Israel: a left-handed, would-be assassin, by the name of Ehud. God had raised him up for such a time as this—and not just for a scoreboard victory. This wasn't about property line expansion or bragging rights; this was all about a curse being shattered by the hand of God.

> "But when the children of Israel cried out to the Lord, the Lord raised up a deliverer for them: Ehud the son of Gera, the Benjamite, a left-handed man. By him the children of Israel sent tribute to Eglon king of Moab" (Judges 3:15).

In this particular time in history, the deliverer would take the shape of a judge, a Benjamite, a lefty. One who had little battlefield experience, but one whom God had placed His hand upon. The 500-year-old Moabite curse would be broken, because God raised up a deliverer. This story is incredible with all the complexities and nuances of intrigue and mystery inherent in it, but it really happened. It all came down to a curse, a deliverer, and faithful people, willing to walk in God's promise.

Many of the bad things that happen to us in our lives have nothing at all to do with the Devil.

I remember when I was redeemed from the curse of sin over my own life. For several years, as a teenager running from God, I felt the weight of my own sin. I had run as far as I could. I finally came to the end of myself and realized there wasn't a better plan than God's plan. I had sat tight-fisted through many a church service. I had heard every Bible story known to man and sat with arms folded through countless altar calls. One day though, I finally realized God's unstoppable love just wouldn't let me go! I responded to a salvation invitation on a Sunday morning and kneeled down beside an old-fashioned altar. There, on my knees beside that altar, years of guilt, sin, and ungodliness began to wash off me, layer by layer. I cried what seemed to be rivers of tears releasing all my pent-up guilt and shame. What an incredibly liberating feeling; the curse of sin had been broken!

A Purpose in the Pain

What I'm about to say may seem a little controversial to some, but what I've learned is this: Many of the bad things that happen to us in our lives have nothing at all to do with the Devil. Sometimes the hard places of our life have everything to do with God. You might be asking, "Are you saying God does bad things to us on purpose?" Well, it depends what you mean by "bad things." If those "bad things" shape us and force us into a place of right relationship with God, then yes, He is not above bringing a little pain into our lives to get us to think about our current condition. Remember, the Moabites were a problem for Israel because *God strengthened them.*

> "And the children of Israel again did evil in the sight of the Lord. So the Lord strengthened Eglon king of Moab against Israel, because they had done evil in the sight of the Lord" (Judges 3:12).

Not only did God strengthen Eglon, He strengthened him *against* Israel. God's plan was to bring the people through a season of hardship and personal trial. He wanted them to experience what it was like to live without being under the shadow of His blessing and favor. He wanted them to realize that the good life they had experienced thus far, was because of His mercy being poured out upon their lives. They began to take what God was doing for them for granted and began to drift towards evil. The people of God were worshiping idols and living in ways that were displeasing to God. The Lord raised up a people against them, but His endgame was not pain. God's ultimate purpose for them was for them to experience absolute freedom from the curse of sin, and yes, the curse of Moab also.

There is nothing like pain or a sense of desperation to force us to call out to God. Israel cried out to the Lord because they were frustrated, hurt, and just plain tired of living in bondage. They were living under a curse, but that curse was ready to be broken as soon as someone would rise up and truly believe in God. Why did it take a full eighteen years for Israel to be set free from Moabite bondage? The reason is simple: That's how long it took for the people to cry out to the Lord in desperation. That time frame could have been much shorter or longer, but the contingency wasn't God's; it was the people's choice.

Great Walls are Made for Great Falls

In Bible times, cities that were fortresses of strength or military power were called strongholds. A stronghold in those days could be pretty intimidating to look at from a military point of view. A stronghold usually had a fortified wall built around it. This was meant to control who came in and who went out. There was also a certain mystique to this, as people were unable to tell exactly what was behind that intimidating wall. Strongholds also exist outside of the biblical context of ancient war. A stronghold can be anything in our lives that is a source of pain or difficult to manage. A personal stronghold is called a "stronghold" for a reason: It is strong, meaning it is not easy to defeat or overcome, and can become a lifelong issue if not dealt with properly.

A stronghold can be anything in our lives that is a source of pain or difficult to manage.

Over my years of ministry, I have dealt with many people who have experienced great strongholds in their lives. Some of them take the form of addiction, anger, insecurity, rejection, and more. I know God has the power to break any stronghold that exists over a believer's life; He is waiting for an Ehud to rise up and walk in His authority to overcome those strongholds.

> "For the weapons of our warfare are not carnal but mighty in God for pulling down strongholds" (2 Corinthians 10:4).

Ehud was used by God to break the curse because Ehud allowed God to use him. It wasn't that he was the only possible candidate, but God saw something in Him worth investing in. Verse 15 tells us: "the Lord raised up a deliverer for them: Ehud the son of Gera." God loves to use ordinary people just like you and me to do His will. Yes, Ehud was raised up by God, but so are you!

I preached a sermon years ago entitled, "Great walls are made for great falls!" It was a message built around the story of Jericho found in the book of Joshua. The walls of this stronghold city were thick and impenetrable, but God had a plan. His plan wasn't to find a warrior who would scale the wall and create havoc inside. His plan wasn't to dig a massive tunnel underneath or even carry a Trojan horse into the city. His plan involved an obedient army of people who would simply walk around the city. They would walk and at the appropriate time, the priests would blow the trumpets and the people would shout. Their walking around the city was an act of faith in God. It was a silent decree that their trust was in the Lord and in Him alone.

God can crush any stronghold, but He chooses to use people like us to do it!

As they walked around the city, it was an expression of their confidence, in the fact that the Almighty would do for them what they could not do for themselves. It was His plan, His power, and His strength, but it utilized their obedience. The stronghold of Jericho represented a massive and overwhelming obstacle, but this challenge was of no consequence when confronted by the power of God. He alone would destroy the walls of the city, but God's people still played a vital role. God can crush any stronghold, but He chooses to use people like us to do it!

As the Israelites marched around the city over and over for days on end, I can almost hear their frustration. Why are we doing this again? What exactly is supposed to be happening here? Is this the actual plan or are we doing something a little more tangible? It wasn't their strength that would bring down the walls, but their obedience. On the final day and on the final pass around the city, something incredible happened.

> "So the people shouted when the priests blew the trumpets. And it happened when the people heard the sound of the trumpet, and the people shouted with a great shout, that the wall fell down flat. Then the people went up into the city, every man straight before him, and they took the city" (Joshua 6:20).

God followed through on what He said He would do. He had promised Joshua victory, but that victory was contingent on their obedience. The strongholds we face in our lives, though intimidating and seemingly impenetrable, are no match for God either! Your insecurities, your pain and hurt from past experiences, your difficulty with rejection: all of these areas can be overcome through God's power. Remember, obedience is the key!

When Ehud faced King Eglon, his Moabite stronghold, and the oppressive 500-year-old curse, his victory came about because he was obedient to God. Just as Israel defeated Jericho and Ehud led Israel to conquer Moab, God will use you to conquer the strongholds in your life and help others conquer theirs as well. The curse of strongholds is broken through the power of Christ.

> "As you therefore have received Christ Jesus the Lord, so walk in Him" (Colossians 2:6).

Walking in Him is more than a cute little prayer or an occasional Sunday morning church service. Walking in Him means complete obedience to Him, and willingness to follow wherever He leads. For Ehud, the left-handed assassin, this required complete sold-out obedience to God's plan. It required nerves of steel and a steady hand, but this stronghold would be broken because God said it would be broken.

THE CURSE BROKEN

Sometimes we settle in areas of our lives that have been disheveled for far too long. We think, *It's always been this way!* If we believe something cannot change, we do not try to change it; we just stop. There are many mindsets that could be listed here: *My family has always had problems with money. My family is known to have anger issues. My family has always been prone to marital strife.* These things may even be true, but they don't have to remain true. It's time to break the curses; it's time for Ehuds to rise up and say, "We will no longer be bound by a Moabite curse." Five hundred years is a very long time: too long to be bound, broken, and cursed. I believe God is ready to set people free from various bondages in their lives. He is the ultimate curse breaker!

Jesus, standing in the synagogue on the Sabbath, began to read from the book of Isaiah. He was prophesying about Himself. He read,

> "The Spirit of the Lord is upon Me, because He has anointed Me to preach the gospel to the poor; He has sent Me to heal the brokenhearted, to proclaim liberty to the captives and recovery of sight to the blind, to set at liberty those who are oppressed" (Luke 4:18).

Jesus is still declaring this to believers today. He is the bondage breaker. There is power in the name of Jesus that can shatter and revoke any bondage you have in your life. Sin is removed in Jesus, and all healing: emotional, physical, and spiritual is subject to His authority.

The strongholds in your life have no other choice than to respond to the power in the name of Jesus!

Believers, hear me, your God is stronger than anything you will ever face. There is no devil big enough or circumstance great enough to keep God's power at bay. The strongholds in your life have no other choice than to respond to the power in the name of Jesus! Declare victory over your life, walk in obedience to the Lord, declare and decree God's greatness, and watch those strongholds come down. Great walls are made for great falls.

Chapter 3: He Who Praises

Chapter 3: He Who Praises

Imagine for a moment that you receive an invitation to a birthday party for one of your close colleagues. After shopping for days, you finally make a decision on the perfect present. You have some idea of this person's interests and you feel you have done a great job in honoring them. On the evening of the party, you choose just the right outfit, one that is classy, but won't take the attention off the birthday girl. You drive to the party with great anticipation and as you arrive you take special care that you are not noticed so you don't spoil the surprise. As you sit in your vehicle you wonder, *Who else is coming? How large is this party going to be?* You have no idea.

You make your way from your car into the room designated on the invitation. As you walk into the room, you can't help but notice the lavish decorations which attest to the great amount of time put into this momentous occasion. You see a table at the side of the room piled high with presents, a carving station and a serving line for a spectacular meal. You even notice there is a band playing softly in the corner of the room. Clearly money was no object for this big birthday surprise.

You begin to make your way around the room and greet your friends and coworkers. The band continues to play in the background and dinner is served. It is a fun and festive birthday celebration. People begin to step up to a microphone and make kind comments about the birthday girl politely followed by warm applause. As you look around the room you begin to feel concerned though. Where is the birthday girl? You were so impressed with the decorations, food, presents, and music, that you somehow missed the actual focus of the party. Where is she? Is she somewhere in the back, listening in and planning to make an appearance at just the right time?

You finally walk over to one of your coworkers who you knew was involved in the planning and ask them the question: "Hey, where is the birthday girl?" You see a look of disappointment cross their face and quickly realize something isn't right. To your disbelief, you are informed that the guest of honor was unable to attend! What? Is it possible that after all this preparation and expense, the person the party was prepared for wasn't even there? What kind of party was this? Why would we honor a person who could not even enjoy the fact that they were being celebrated? In this scenario, the party was a celebration for the attendees, not the birthday girl herself.

Keeping the Right Focus

The focus of our lives is constantly under attack. Just like in the story of the birthday party mix up, it is common for people to expend energy on things that are of little value. Even with our best intentions to stay focused on the Lord, it is easy for us to get off track and make our relationship more focused on what we can receive instead of what we can give. Ehud was a man of incredible focus; we know this because he stayed the course from the beginning planning stages all the way to the successful end of his assignment. The name *Ehud* means "he who praises"[4] and I believe this was the key to his success.

We get a little snippet of Ehud's thinking and belief system immediately after the assassination of the Moabite king. Ehud, coming off a successful operation, and still on the high of his adrenaline-rushed success, now addresses the men of the nation. It would have been easy for him to say, "Look at what I have done!" Instead he is careful to turn the attention to the Lord. When he speaks to the people, he could have pointed to his own bravery, or his willingness to do what nobody else had done for almost

4. "Biblical baby names starting with 'e'," Biblical baby names starting with e - Page 2, accessed October 05, 2017, http://www.sheknows.com/baby-names/biblical-baby-names/browse/e/page:2.

two decades. When he has the attention of the Hebrew leadership, he makes this statement:

> "Then he said to them, 'Follow me, for the *Lord* has delivered your enemies the Moabites into your hand.' So they went down after him, seized the fords of the Jordan leading to Moab, and did not allow anyone to cross over" (Judges 3:28).

From birth, Ehud was called "he who praises." As he heard his name over and over throughout his lifetime, it was a constant reminder of the necessity to give God His due praise. In Scripture, we see the significance of names and the prophetic ramifications they carried. This man was not born to be an ordinary man, but a man of extravagant praise.

Chewing the Cud

To really understand the power of praise in this story, it is necessary to look back just a bit farther, to the circumstances through which Ehud was named.

> "But when the children of Israel cried out to the *Lord*, the *Lord* raised up a deliverer for them: Ehud the son of Gera, the Benjamite, a left-handed man" (Judges 3:15, *emphasis mine*).

Ehud was the son of Gera; in Hebrew, the name *Gera* literally means, "to chew the cud."[5] As you may know, cattle have a very complicated digestive system. From what I've been told, a cow will actually regurgitate their food and chew it again. This chewing of partially digested food is known as chewing the cud. If you've ever driven past a cow pasture and witnessed this, you'll know what I'm referring to, but it isn't uncommon to see a cow just standing and staring off into space and chewing. What are they doing? You guessed it: They are

5. Gordon Wilton, "Book of Judges Bible Study - The Message of Judges: Chapter Three, Ehud, the Fat Man and the Power of Praise!" Book of Judges Bible Study - Ehud and the power of praise, accessed October 05, 2017, http://www.jesusplusnothing.com/studies/online/judges6.htm.

chewing the cud! It may seem odd to name someone after this, but on deeper inspection this idea could be used to describe meditation too. Not the meditation we see in the New Age Movement, but meditation that focuses on the Lord and what He is saying to us.

> "Blessed is the man who walks not in the counsel of the ungodly, nor stands in the path of sinners, nor sits in the seat of the scornful; but his delight is in the law of the Lord, and in His law he meditates day and night. He shall be like a tree planted by the rivers of water, that brings forth its fruit in its season, whose leaf also shall not wither; and whatever he does shall prosper" (Psalm 1:1-3).

The psalmist declares strength and fruitfulness flowing forth from those who meditate on God's Word and His goodness. Gera (to chew the cud) is a true symbol of careful and calculated decision-making, based on meditation in God's Word. Think about this for a moment: "Gera, (to chew the cud), was the father of Ehud, (he that praises)." I believe it could accurately be said that meditation on God's Word will give birth to powerful praise.

In our seasons of pain, sorrow, adversity, and confusion, it is very easy to lose sight of our praise. When we force ourselves to be focused on the Lord, praise is a natural outflow of that commitment. God doesn't get confused. He doesn't run out of answers, and He surely never loses. Regardless of how bad things appear to be, meditation on the Lord and His goodness will give birth to significant, and situation-altering praise!

We don't have a lot of background information on Ehud, as this story gets very little press coverage in the Bible. I have to believe that praise was more than just an attribute of his name; I believe it defined who he was. I can see a man giving praise to God as he felt the overwhelming weight of responsibility in carrying the people of Israel. He knew that he could no longer wait on someone else to do what he had the burden and ability to do himself. In that time of feeling that heavy responsibility, he turned his attention to the Lord. This was not just a slight advantage for him, it was the key to his success.

Becoming a Warrior

In life, we are dealt a hand of cards, so to speak. In this "game" of life, we may not like the hand we've been given, but it is our hand. It's easy to look at other people's lives and their situations, and think, *I wish I had their life.* That is, however, impossible. "It is what it is" as the saying goes. I want to encourage you to stop and think, though: *Is the hand I've been dealt just a momentary obstacle?* Could it be that God has allowed certain situations to occur in your life because He knew you would not only overcome them, but come out on the other side of them victorious and stronger for having been through them? Ehud wasn't born a successful warrior; he became one as a result of the "hand" he was dealt. He was undiscovered until opportunity met his potential. In his anxiety and uncertainty, Ehud continued his praise. I am reminded of another biblical warrior who was also a man of unlikely origin, yet had great success: David, the son of Jesse.

> God has allowed certain situations to occur in your life because He knew you would not only overcome them, but come out on the other side of them victorious and stronger.

You remember him: the David who defeated Goliath. He was many things in life. He was a shepherd, a giant killer, a faithful and trusted advisor to King Saul, a successful warrior, and eventually a king himself. At the heart of who David was though, was something much deeper than titles and accomplishments. David was a man of worship.

While reflecting about God's plan over Israel, the Apostle Paul preaching in the synagogue, stated:

> "And when He had removed him, He raised up for them David as king, to whom also He gave testimony and

> said, 'I have found David the son of Jesse, a man after My own heart, who will do all My will'" (Acts 13:22).

David was a man after God's own heart. What does that mean? Was David just a well-intentioned person who caught a few lucky breaks or was it something much deeper? You can see the source of David's strength woven throughout the worship he wrote in the Psalms. He had an incredible love for God, but his love was deepened in worship. Worship was more than an expression of David's love for God; it was a means of deepening that love.

Once after David went through some intense challenges and a near death experience, he sought refuge among the Philistines, hiding from King Saul. Everything was going fine until some of the Philistines recognized David as the one who had defeated Goliath years before. David was reported to the king of the region as a secret spy, a mole placed by the Hebrews to defeat the Philistines. This, of course, wasn't true, but it forced David to act in order to preserve his own life. David did what any normal person would do at a time like this. He pretended to be crazy. Not just a little off, but stark raving mad! He went all out, spit running down his beard, clawing at the city gates, and howling with insanity. He acted so crazy that it quickly drew the attention of the Philistine's upper echelon. As wild as it sounds, it actually worked. The king not only spared David's life, but kicked him out of town, as he had no need for any additional crazy folk.

Building a Testimony

Now, David was in a real bind. He had been running from Saul for months and was absolutely worn out. The one place he thought he could find refuge was nearly fatal too. David retreated to the cave of Adullam. This was no ordinary cave; this was a cave that overlooked the valley of Elah in which David defeated Goliath years before. David had come back full circle to where it all began when he was a young shepherd boy. Looking out over the valley that had once been the highlight of his life, David had a choice to make. He could be crushed by the circumstances he found himself in, or he could turn His attention to the Lord. The name *Adullam* means, "their testimony; their prey; their ornament."[6]

> Out of the hardest places come the greatest testimonies.

David was building a testimony, a testimony that would come out of a hard place, a testimony unlike anyone else's. Out of the hardest places come the greatest testimonies. Your hard place may look like a dead-end road right now, a place that lies somewhere between an old washed-up valley of victory and a cave of seclusion. This is the very place where greatness is born! Satan would have loved nothing more than for this cave to be David's final resting place: a place of broken promises, and the demise of Israel's most promising warrior. But David's action in this moment would forever mold his destiny.

David could have cried out an exasperating shout of surrender or David could choose to carry on. You already know what he did, but it goes deeper than just this simple choice. David had already seen his share of difficulty in the past, and he knew the secret to success. It wasn't another political ploy, or hoping to be lucky enough to have some chance encounter that would buy him another day. David's success was tied to his praise. I believe, while standing at the mouth of that cave, designed to kill him, David uttered the words that would carry him for the remainder of his life.

> "I will bless the Lord at all times; His praise shall continually be in my mouth. My soul shall make its boast in the Lord; the humble shall hear of it and be glad. Oh, magnify the Lord with me, and let us exalt His name together" (Psalm 34:1-3).

6. Hitchcock, "Adullam," Topical Bible: Adullam, accessed October 05, 2017, http://biblehub.com/topical/a/adullam.htm.

David knew his future depended on the Lord's hand of favor over his life. When he could have given up, he dug deeper. When he could have allowed his enemies to shut him up, it made his praise open up even more. David said, "I will bless the Lord at all times." Did you catch that simple phrase? "I will": praise is always subject to our will. The Enemy can't stop you from what you "will" to do. When you are hurting, you don't feel much like worshiping, but a strong will and focus will say, "I will bless the Lord at all times." David didn't praise the Lord only after he killed giants, outsmarted his adversaries, and defeated his enemies; he praised the Lord at all times!

We normally find it pretty easy to praise and worship God when everything seems to be going our way. What about when your life is so confusing that you feel like a clown juggling bowling pins? You spend your every waking moment trying to keep all those pins in the air, but on your best day, things keep crashing to the ground. It's during these seasons, these moments of pain and desperation, that our praise benefits us most. Your true identity as a person of praise isn't revealed in the good seasons of life, it's revealed when everything is coming unraveled.

Your true identity as a person of praise isn't revealed in the good seasons of life, it's revealed when everything is coming unraveled.

Worship Brings Breakthrough

I've seen it over and over again: People are able to walk into some of the greatest breakthroughs of their lives during worship. I've watched people come into our church, hurt, downcast, and carrying the weight of the world on their shoulders, and then they begin to worship. There's something powerful that happens in worship; it's in that place where the majesty of God is revealed. When we have a brief reprieve from our pain, and get our eyes on Him, the stress, pain, and anxiety begins to lift.

Fussing and complaining comes easily to most of us. It is simply a natural response to the pressure we are experiencing or the struggle we are enduring. Ehud had a lot to fuss about. Remember, he was part of a nation that had been oppressed and in bondage for an eighteen-year period. There were adult people walking around who had never known the taste of living in a free nation. Ehud could have complained and shaken his fist at God, but that would have been against his nature because he was a man of praise.

Ehud was born to be a man of powerful worship and dedication to the Lord. His success in life as a judge, assassin, and warrior didn't come by chance. His success came from the Lord, but was received through his praise. I'm sure the hard challenges of his life seemed overwhelming at the time, but His praise opened the door for the supernatural to take place.

Just over two years ago, my family and I walked through a situation that would forever change our lives. My wife, Michelle, went to her regularly scheduled annual exam complete with mammogram. They noticed a small irregularity and decided that a biopsy was necessary. We were obviously concerned, but we had great faith in God and were confident that He wouldn't allow anything serious to happen to us. After all, we pastored an influential church, were involved in international ministry, and were being faithful to everything we believed God was asking of us.

Well, the results came back and it was cancer, the one diagnosis we had dreaded most. She was diagnosed with stage two breast cancer, and would need to have surgery and immediate subsequent treatments. To say we were absolutely shocked would be an understatement. I looked over at my beautiful wife as we received the news and I distinctly remember feeling utterly helpless. I'll be honest with you, I questioned God. I remember saying in my head, *God, are You serious? After all we've given to the ministry and to the kingdom, this is what we get?*

I'll never forget that feeling; it was a surreal experience. We were in such shock that it felt like we were hovering above the room and looking down on this happening to someone other than us. The first thought that popped into my mind and that I almost said to the doctor was: *Do you know who we are?* I was quickly checked by the Holy Spirit and felt Him speak to me saying, "Do you know who I am?" In that moment, we chose to put our trust in the Lord, but it was not without a battle.

My own emotions as well as my wife's were flooded by this attack of the Enemy. The very core of our faith would be challenged; the Enemy's plan was to cause us to quit and ultimately destroy us. I'll never forget the night we sat down with our three kids and told them the news. Michelle was sitting on the bed; I was kneeling beside the bed, and the kids were gathered around in different parts of the room. I told them what the doctor said, then I told them what we would believe God to do. That night, crushed in the natural, as a family joined together, we prayed the prayer of faith over my wife. We began to praise God and thank Him for seeing us through this situation, and building a powerful testimony.

A week or so later, we would meet with some additional doctors and receive their recommendations. One of the doctors we met with was a medical oncologist who specialized in chemotherapy. We were praying and believing that chemotherapy would be unnecessary. The need for chemo was dependent upon the tumor's size; there was a cutoff. If the tumor was small enough, chemo would not be necessary. We had heard some horror stories of sickness and hair loss and decided we didn't want any part of that. The night before the consultation my wife and I decided to celebrate. You heard right, the night before; we hadn't even consulted yet. We went out and had a nice steak, baked potato and all the accompaniments. Our plan was to give God praise in advance, before we even heard the good news.

On the following day, we met with the specialist and our worst fears were confirmed. She would need extensive chemotherapy and radiation following surgery. Our celebratory dinner had not been not in vain; it was just that the ultimate healing would be delayed. Again, we had a choice, and we chose to place our confidence in the Lord by praising Him anyway. During her treatments, we stayed very intentional and focused on giving God praise in the middle of the storm. We recited Psalm 34:1-3 over and over, so much so that it became our "theme psalm."

I printed out a list of healing Scriptures and Michelle made copies of them and put them all around our bedroom. On our mirror above the sink, over her vanity area, in the bathroom, where she does her makeup, by the bedside, all over the place. We wanted to intentionally create an atmosphere of faith.

> "So then faith comes by hearing, and hearing by the word of God" (Romans 10:17).

Each night, we prayed together and spoke God's healing word over her body. In every prayer, on every night, we gave praise to the Lord for being faithful to His Word.

When you choose to give God praise, regardless of what you're facing, it sets you up for great victory.

The fight on our hands would prove to be long and exhausting. We would have to travel about an hour and a half every single weekday for six weeks of radiation treatments. The chemo was physically exhausting and emotionally draining; the treatment was administered once every three weeks for a five-month period. After chemo treatments, my wife would be in bed for two or three days. During all of this, we were still leading an explosive church, complete with all the drama and excitement that entails. Our church people were unbelievably compassionate and helpful to us. People began to bring food to our house; they were signed up for weeks on end. People even took special requests from our kids about their favorite dishes. There was a group of ladies that began to meet and have prayer meetings, specifically for Michelle. The church rallied together and became a great support system for us. We really felt

God's love through our own church people as they became the hands and feet of Jesus extended to us and walking with us through this trial.

Through the fatigue, uncertainty, and crazy schedules, we knew we had to continue to give praise to the Lord. My wife is an amazing person; I'm sure she had some questions for the Lord, but she never expressed them, if she did. She was careful to always speak faith, and to always give praise to God, both publicly and privately. Michelle has always been a woman of great faith, but I began to see something rise up in her that was even stronger than before. In this long journey, God was building something that could never be destroyed. He was building a testimony from our faith and our experience that would have been impossible, without the specifics of this path. I'm not saying that if we were given the option, we would have chosen this path, but God has truly worked on our behalf to make us better, stronger, and more fearless. Our faith, the faith of our church people, and the faith of our children, was made stronger as a result of this journey.

Out of all this, a powerful ministry was born. When you choose to give God praise, regardless of what you're facing, it sets you up for great victory. Right after Michelle's successful bout with breast cancer, the Lord put a powerful ministry in her heart: to come alongside cancer patients and help them become people of praise too. She designed a special box that would include items of particular interest for cancer patients. One of the items in that box is the list of healing Scriptures that we prayed over her for many months when we were in the middle of our storm.

These boxes have been given out to families all over the nation and we are getting constant reports of how God has used our praise as a blessing to others. When you put the Lord on a pedestal of praise, there is a drawing to His greatness. For us, it was the healing of a dreaded disease. Praise God! Michelle has had two mammograms since her treatment and is clear from any trace of cancer! God's design was that our healing would become a source of strength and encouragement for others in similar situations. None of this could have happened without a steady flow of praise to God.

Choosing to Praise

In every situation in which you find yourself, you have a choice. You can choose to either magnify your pain or you can choose to magnify the Lord. In Psalm 34:3, David says, "Come magnify the Lord with me, let us exalt his name together." At the time of this writing, this wasn't the easy choice for David; but in the end, David was not only delivered from his enemies, but he was able to stand in a permanent place of victory over them. Notice he says, "Let us." David is welcoming others to join him in this. Your praise is contagious! Just like murmuring and complaining can spread like wildfire, so can praise. I'd much rather be around a group of people giving praise to God, than those griping about their problems any day of the week!

In every situation in which you find yourself, you have a choice. You can choose to either magnify your pain or you can choose to magnify the Lord.

Ehud was a man restricted to a life of bondage and oppression. He could easily have joined in with the chorus of complainers. Instead he chose to lead by being a man of intentional praise. I'm glad he chose the latter! I'm glad, not just because it makes for a good story, but because it makes for a good example.

I can hear him now, on the way to the king's chambers to carry his tribute money, humming songs of praise under his breath. In his mind, all the way into his private meeting, God was the center of Ehud's plan. When he was successful, his natural response was to give God the glory for the victory he had seen. Ehud was born to be a man of praise, and a man of praise he was. He praised God when was in bondage to a Moabite madman, and he praised God when he led the nation to victory over that very same man.

My challenge to you today is this: Become a person of praise. Being that person will most likely go against everything you feel like doing. Your fleshly nature is not naturally prone to praise. In the natural, we are prone to say exactly what we feel. If we're tired, sad, hungry, lonely, discouraged, or whatever, we verbalize those exact sentiments. A person of praise though filters their statements through the depth of the faith they carry. The flesh wants to react, whereas the faith responds. Our faith needs to be encouraged and pulled up from within us intentionally. Jesus provides a great example of this in His last few hours on the earth. While in the garden of Gethsemane, with the weight of impending death, He gathers with His disciples for one final prayer meeting. Jesus knew He would need all the spiritual and physical strength possible to see His mission to completion. He would carry the sin of the world, and He would die a horrible physical death. The entirety of His public ministry had now culminated in this final gathering. It is here we get a glimpse of what a true person of praise really looks like.

> "And He was withdrawn from them about a stone's throw, and He knelt down and prayed, saying, 'Father, if it is Your will, take this cup away from Me; nevertheless not My will, but Yours, be done'" (Luke 22:41-42).

Even in the face of imminent torture and eventual death, Jesus turned the attention to His Father. It would have been easy to cry out in His own pain: "Why Me? This is more than I can handle; please God, don't make Me do this!" But Jesus, the ultimate man of praise, says, "not My will, but Yours, be done." In this act of self-denial and focused praise, Jesus points to the Lord. What a valuable lesson for us! In our darkest and most difficult times, we need to praise the Lord, not just for Him, but for us. Look at what came out of Jesus' obedience to God, made possible by His praise: The redemption of humanity! I'm so thankful for His example.

The true last day warriors for the Lord will be people of praise. The complainers and bellyachers will never lead a move of God, but the worshipers will. Be intentional about your praise, and purpose yourself to praise Him in every circumstance. Bless the Lord at all times and watch God bless you in all things.

> In our darkest and most difficult times, we need to praise the Lord, not just for Him, but for us.

At the beginning of this chapter, we began with a scenario involving a birthday party with no guest of honor. In life, there are many ups and downs, many detours, and many opportunities to get bitter. There are also many opportunities to get stronger and believe deeper. Our life can be one great celebration, but that doesn't mean there is no pain. It simply means that when Jesus is the true guest of honor, the celebration isn't for us; it is for Him. Make your praise intentional; stay focused on Jesus; like Ehud, be "he who praises."

Chapter 4: Eight Seconds

Chapter 4: Eight Seconds

I have two sons, and both of them have always been obsessed with anything and everything that would be considered dangerous weaponry. From knives to ninja stars, swords, guns, you name it: it's all intriguing to them. They have always liked movies with battle scenes, and of course, the role-playing of battle in the house. Although some of the brotherly battles were real, the majority were just noisy pretending. When I say noisy, I do mean noisy, complete with sound effects and sometimes the crash of breaking furniture or other items from around the house.

I remember one night in particular. My wife and I were asleep in our bedroom and were awakened by the sound of breaking glass. I immediately sprang to my feet to protect the family, and went running into the living room, expecting to confront a burglar. What I found instead were two boys "sword-fighting" with a couple of brooms. In their epic battle, they had knocked a mirror off the wall and were quickly trying to hide the evidence. They were unsuccessful at the cover-up, but this experience does underscore the thinking of juvenile boys.

What is it about weapons that fascinates boys (of all ages)? Is it the potential devastation that can be unleashed, or is it something within them that just loves the thought of holding something so powerful? Whatever the reason, there is a strong attraction to things that have to be handled with proper supervision.

The Dagger

Ehud's only weapon was a simple dagger. The Bible does tell us how this particular weapon came about:

> "Now Ehud made himself a dagger (it was double-edged and a cubit in length) and fastened it under his clothes on his right thigh" (Judges 3:16).

The dagger Ehud carried into the king's chamber wasn't something he picked up at a local pawn shop. He actually fashioned it himself. He would have had to have found the right piece of metal and cut it to the specific dimensions he needed. In ancient times, a cubit was the distance from the elbow to the fingertips or roughly eighteen inches.[7] Ehud was very specific and intentional about his plans. It is obvious that his mission to assassinate King Eglon was not a knee-jerk reaction. He worked for it and planned it for a long time.

This dagger had to be perfect. There would be absolutely no room for error, as any mistake here would be fatal. He had one chance, one shot, to kill the king; if anything went wrong, the king's bodyguards would surround him and they would surely kill him. How long does it take to make a dagger? I'm no expert in making daggers, but I am pretty sure this took quite a bit of time, probably months. Nothing less than perfection would do; he had no choice but to get this right the first time. I'm sure he spent countless hours sharpening the steel, sanding the handle, cutting down the steel to a smaller size, fashioning a holster of some sort. Perhaps, just as it was approaching completion, he saw a small flaw and began the process of sanding, grinding, and sharpening this important blade all over again.

Ehud knew there would be no second chances. His life and the lives of his Hebrew brothers and sisters were at stake. Failure was not an option and his success would depend on one word: preparation. You might be thinking; "I'm sure the actual attack plan was more time consuming

7. Bodie Hodge, "How Long Was the Original Cubit?" Answers in Genesis, April 01, 2007, accessed October 05, 2017, https://answersingenesis.org/noahs-ark/how-long-was-the-original-cubit/.

and important than the weapon itself." As true as that might be, if the weapon failed, all the planning would be for nothing. Ehud probably spent long hours rehearsing and thinking about exactly how he would assassinate Eglon. As he was sharpening the blade, sweat poured down his face and onto the steel blade as his mind raced to the king's chamber where he knew he would eventually stand. Ehud's thoughts probably sounded something like this: *I have to get this right, I cannot mess up. There's no room for error. I have to be prepared.*

Failure was not an option and his success would depend on one word: preparation.

Some things in life appear to be just a blip on a screen. As a minister, I officiate many weddings. Most of the ceremonies last for forty-five minutes or less. Weeks are spent by the couple-to-be, picking out a wedding venue, reception hall, and caterer. More time still is spent in developing a guest list, finding the perfect dress, and choosing the theme for the wedding itself. This ceremony ties people together legally, and will hopefully last for many years. However, the ceremony is short. Forty-five minutes to herald something that lasts a lifetime. Much of what we do is actually preparing us for the future ahead. On the other hand, many things require intense preparation while the actual event is over quickly. One example of this is the wild, wooly sport of bull-riding.

Bull-riding is a very popular sport all across the South, and is actually carried on major sports channels multiple times a year. I've never had the guts to actually ride a bull, but I certainly admire the guys who do. It looks extremely dangerous, yet it is precise, and requires incredible skill, strength, and persistence. One wrong move and someone could be easily crushed beneath the weight of a 2,000-pound angry bull!

I've heard of bull riders going to great lengths in order to train their bodies for the brutal ride awaiting them on an unruly beast. They train for strength, flexibility, agility and more. One bad ride could be their final ride. Competitive bull riding is a contest in which the rider is judged on his balance, fluidity, hand placement, and more. Even the bull is judged on how aggressive of a ride they provide. Bull riding is judged on a hundred-point scale and all of these things and more are taken into account.[8]

Imagine a rodeo, full of people wearing big cowboy hats, boots, and tight jeans. The stands are crowded with eager fans, all there to cheer on their bull-riding hopefuls. As the rider approaches the chute, the bull begins to snort and stamp his feet on the freshly turned dirt. The smell of popcorn, peanuts, and hot dogs fill the air, and the countdown is on for the next ride. The rider is seated on the bull that begins to twist and move under the unwelcome weight, and the bull immediately begins to "size up" the rider, planning how he will throw him off his back. The bull rider adjusts his grip on the rope and mentally prepares himself for the wild ride that is about to ensue. The gate swings open and the clock begins to tick. What seems like a very short amount of time to the spectator is quite long for that rider. If the rider can keep his bearings and stay on until the buzzer sounds, he will be rewarded with a high score. If not, he suffers a harsh fall to the ground, and can quickly become prey to a furious beast.

The bull rider must stay on this wild, untamed, bucking, angry bull for eight full seconds. Can you imagine that? Months or years of training converge, and in the end it all comes down to an eight-second contest. If he doesn't make it the full eight seconds, he receives no score for that ride at all! It must be a huge letdown to train for months and then fall short by a few seconds or less. All of that preparation, dedication, and training for eight seconds!

As Ehud approached King Eglon and pulled his dagger, I think it was the same. The whole assassination probably lasted somewhere in the vicinity of eight seconds. Like a bull rider, his training, contemplation, strategy, and weaponry all came down to an eight-second window!

8. "Scoring and Judging," Professional Bull Riders, accessed October 05, 2017, http://www.pbr.com/en/education/scoring_and_judging.aspx.

Things had the potential to go really good, or they had the potential to be really bad. Thankfully, the preparation and dedication of Ehud was thorough and rewarded with great success.

Much of the successes we have aren't realized in actual achievement, but in the preparation that led to those achievements. When we see the athletic "greats" out on the field, we see examples of those who had laser-focused determination to be the very best they could be. A sports team that wins a championship or rises to any level of difficult accomplishment didn't reach that pinnacle of success without painstaking preparation.

Much of the successes we have aren't realized in actual achievement, but in the preparation that led to those achievements.

In the mid-90s, I loved watching my favorite athlete. The playoffs couldn't arrive soon enough. I could not wait to cheer for my idol, Michael Jordan, when he was on the court. It seemed like he could almost fly, demolishing the competition game after game. He made being a basketball star look so easy, yet we know that very few ever attain to that level of play. Jordan stands in history as being one of the best players of all time, but he didn't get to that level easily.

Jordan had a reputation of intense and focused play. He also had the reputation of very strict and difficult workout schedules, both on and off-season. He spent hours in the gym doing strength training, agility training, and shooting endless buckets day after day. When game day came, he was prepared, not just mentally, but in every way. He did not do well because his opponents were fearful of his abilities, but because he had invested his time in practice before the game. Nobody could match him on the court, but his excellence was developed off the court.

When I was a teenager, I played high school football. There was nothing like the smell of grass, dirt, and the stench of a field full of sweaty athletes. I loved it! I can remember hour upon hour of running, lifting, and preparing for a Friday night game. During football season it seemed like our lives were dedicated to the sport. My coach constantly repeated this mantra: "You play like you practice." Nothing made him angrier than guys who were lazy in practice and not going full speed. He knew greatness wasn't born on the playing field; it was born on the practice field.

Greatness wasn't born on the playing field;
it was born on the practice field.

As I am writing this chapter, I am in a little city in western Honduras called Cucuyagua. I have the privilege of being able to preach in multiple churches that we oversee, and I am blessed to see the hand of God move in this hungry nation. Tonight I will be preaching in our main campus ministry where there will be several churches gathered together to celebrate the anniversary of the church.

I am not just going to go up to the pulpit and "wing it." I won't step up to the microphone and just hope God gives me the words to say. I have spent much time in preparation for this moment. I take this very seriously, and have prayed and studied intensely so that when I stand behind the pulpit tonight, my preparation will meet His anointing, and God will do what only He can do. You might say, "Well, if you believe God is speaking through you, you really don't need to prepare." I have a responsibility, and my lack of preparation could actually hinder what God wants to do. Not that God has to have me, but He chooses to use me.

Here, surrounded by this beautiful mountainous landscape in Honduras, I feel the weight and responsibility to preach. I do not want to be just speaking from head knowledge, but to preach the Word that comes from deep and sincere preparation. When I begin to minister God's Word, I know He will bring back to my memory those things that I've studied and prepared. Without preparation, I would be speaking from an empty reservoir.

Many weeks ago, I began to pray and study specific passages of Scripture. I studied through each passage by looking at past sermon notes and reading through commentaries on them. I prayed over and over, asking the Lord to direct me as to when and how to speak on each different passage or subject. That preparation created a foundation of ministry readiness that brings forth powerful results when tapped.

We all have similar situations that require us to be spiritually alert and poised for whatever the Enemy may bring against us. Success isn't usually created on the battlefield of our lives; that's just the place where it becomes official.

The Lord spoke to Jeremiah about this concept. God was getting ready to deliver the Babylonians into the hands of the Israelites. Nevertheless, before that could happen there were some requirements on the part of God's people. The Lord told them to prepare, sharpen their arrows, gather their battle supplies, and join with those who were being raised up by the Lord.

> "Make the arrows bright! Gather the shields! The Lord has raised up the spirit of the kings of the Medes. For His plan is against Babylon to destroy it, because it is the vengeance of the Lord, the vengeance for His temple. Set up the standard on the walls of Babylon; make the guard strong, set up the watchmen, prepare the ambushes, for the Lord has both devised and done what He spoke against the inhabitants of Babylon" (Jeremiah 51:11-12).

God was going to make sure the battle was a success, but success was predicated on preparation. God always has a plan; but for it to work in us, we have to cooperate. The Lord didn't just tell the people they would succeed, and that was the end of the story. He didn't just tell them to pray harder and believe more. He gave them specific things to do as an act of faith, so His power would be revealed through them.

I've noticed that crisis prayer can have some benefit, but much of it is unnecessary. If we are prepared spiritually before difficulty arises, we don't have to take time getting ourselves dialed in to what God is trying to teach us. A crisis drives us deep into the presence of the Lord, as our conflict cries out for relief, but what if we are already deep in His presence before an emergency comes up, a crisis arises, or a painful experience erupts? What would have been a "crisis prayer" now becomes simply listening and responding to the voice of the Father.

> If we are prepared spiritually before difficulty arises, we don't have to take time getting ourselves dialed in to what God is trying to teach us.

The Nazirite Vow

The story of Samson teaches us much about spiritual readiness. Samson was born in consecration. Most of us have heard the story of Samson over and over and believe the source of his strength was his hair. Although his hair was an expression of commitment to God, his real strength came from his consecration. Samson's consecration went back in time, even before his birth. His own mother bore him in consecration.

> "Again the children of Israel did evil in the sight of the Lord, and the Lord delivered them into the hand of the Philistines for forty years. Now there was a certain man from Zorah, of the family of the Danites, whose name was Manoah; and his wife was barren and had no children. And the Angel of the Lord appeared to the woman and said to her, 'Indeed now, you are barren and have borne no children, but you shall conceive and bear a son. Now therefore, please be careful not to drink wine or similar drink, and not to eat anything unclean. For behold, you shall conceive and bear a son. And no razor shall come upon his head, for the child shall be a Nazirite to God from the womb; and he shall begin to deliver Israel out of the hand of the Philistines'" (Judges 13:1-5).

Later in the same chapter, it goes a little further to explain her role in this "would-be" deliverer.

> "So the Angel of the Lord said to Manoah, 'Of all that I said to the woman let her be careful. She may not eat anything that comes from the vine, nor may she drink wine or similar drink, nor eat anything unclean. All that I commanded her let her observe'" (Judges 13:13-14).

This consecration commanded to Samson's mother would bring forth a son who would be a bondage breaker for the nation. God knew that deliverance required a sold-out discipline and mandate for consecration. The spiritual truth here is simple: Consecration brings forth strength. When we study this vow, called "the Nazirite vow," we see three main parts according to the command regarding Samson.

Drink No Wine

The first command is to drink no wine or similar drink. I believe this reflects the need for consecration in being clear-minded in addition to the fact that it would not allow a lowering of inhibitions due to chemicals in the body. Even more importantly, wine was mixed with drinking water in those days in order to kill any bacteria or parasites in the water. We see this practice in the New Testament in Paul's admonition to Timothy.

> "No longer drink only water, but use a little wine for your stomach's sake and your frequent infirmities" (1 Timothy 5:23).

The Nazirite however, was called to a higher order or faith. One that was not limited to the scope of human health in the natural understanding, but one that completely embraced a life of faith and dependence upon the Lord. God was saying that He would protect the Nazirite as long as there was a continued commitment and faith.

No Razors

The second command was to never allow a razor to touch Samson's head. Why was this so important? Hair was considered a covering for women, but for men to have long hair was disgraceful. If Samson were going to be cut from a different cloth as a man of faith, he would have to learn how to go against the social and cultural grain around him, in order to be fully dedicated to the Lord. So his hair wasn't the sole source of his strength. It was an outward sign of his deep and lifelong devotion to the Lord.

Never Touch a Dead Body

The third command for the Nazirite as outlined in Numbers was to never touch a dead body.

> "All the days that he separates himself to the Lord he shall not go near a dead body. He shall not make himself unclean even for his father or his mother, for his brother or his sister, when they die, because his separation to God is on his head. All the days of his separation he shall be holy to the Lord" (Numbers 6:6-8).

This was the ultimate sign of consecration. God prohibited the consecrated person from touching anything dead. This, of course, has a spiritual implication: As believers we must run from things that have the potential to bring death into our lives.

When we follow the life of Samson, we see a slow, yet consistent path, of deviating from God's commands. In Judges 14, it can be assumed that Samson spent the week partying and drinking with the Philistines at Tinmah when he gets married. Although Scripture doesn't say that Samson actually partook, we do know that the week-long celebration of marriage certainly involved alcohol, and Samson was in attendance for its entirety.

Samson also violated his vow when he stopped and ate honey from a honeycomb which had formed in the carcass of a dead lion. Judges 14 outlines this story. As Samson was traveling, he became hungry and then ate. His willingness to continually cross the line, ever so slightly, was an indicator that his spiritual readiness was beginning to suffer. You may be reading this and thinking to yourself, *Well, this really isn't that big of a deal.* You have to understand this: Samson's vow wasn't just a simple decision based on a spiritual whim. This was a lifelong commitment that found its inception before his conception.

Samson didn't stop here either. There were additional problems. The famous story in Judges 16 of Samson ripping up the city gates in Gaza, and then carrying them up to the top of a mountain, begins with a rather sinister opening.

> "Now Samson went to Gaza and saw a harlot there, and went in to her. When the Gazites were told, "Samson has come here!" they surrounded the place and lay in wait for him all night at the gate of the city. They were quiet all night, saying, "In the morning, when it is daylight, we will kill him." And Samson lay low till midnight; then he arose at midnight, took hold of the doors of the gate of the city and the two gateposts, pulled them up, bar and all, put them on his shoulders, and carried them to the top of the hill that faces Hebron" (Judges 16:1-3).

Did you catch that? Samson sleeping with a harlot! You may be thinking, *As bad as that is, it's not part of the Nazirite vow, right?* That is incorrect though. A Nazirite wasn't a Nazirite instead of being a Hebrew; he was a Nazirite *in addition to* being a Hebrew. Samson was bound to all of the Hebrew ceremonial, religious, and moral laws by birth; he was bound to the Nazirite vow by choice. This sin went deeper than his commitment as a Nazirite; this sin went against the very God who set him apart as a Hebrew.

This is the beginning to the end of Samson's life.

> "Afterward it happened that he loved a woman in the Valley of Sorek, whose name was Delilah. And the lords

of the Philistines came up to her and said to her, 'Entice him, and find out where his great strength lies, and by what means we may overpower him, that we may bind him to afflict him; and every one of us will give you eleven hundred pieces of silver.'

So Delilah said to Samson, 'Please tell me where your great strength lies, and with what you may be bound to afflict you.' And Samson said to her, 'If they bind me with seven fresh bowstrings, not yet dried, then I shall become weak, and be like any other man.'

"So the lords of the Philistines brought up to her seven fresh bowstrings, not yet dried, and she bound him with them. Now men were lying in wait, staying with her in the room. And she said to him, 'The Philistines are upon you, Samson!' But he broke the bowstrings as a strand of yarn breaks when it touches fire. So the secret of his strength was not known.

"Then Delilah said to Samson, 'Look, you have mocked me and told me lies. Now, please tell me what you may be bound with.' So he said to her, 'If they bind me securely with new ropes that have never been used, then I shall become weak, and be like any other man.' Therefore Delilah took new ropes and bound him with them, and said to him, 'The Philistines are upon you, Samson!' And men were lying in wait, staying in the room. But he broke them off his arms like a thread. Delilah said to Samson, 'Until now you have mocked me and told me lies. Tell me what you may be bound with.' And he said to her, 'If you weave the seven locks of my head into the web of the loom'—

"So she wove it tightly with the batten of the loom, and said to him, 'The Philistines are upon you, Samson!' But he awoke from his sleep, and pulled out the batten and

> the web from the loom. Then she said to him, 'How can you say, "I love you," when your heart is not with me? You have mocked me these three times, and have not told me where your great strength lies.' And it came to pass, when she pestered him daily with her words and pressed him, so that his soul was vexed to death, that he told her all his heart, and said to her, 'No razor has ever come upon my head, for I have been a Nazirite to God from my mother's womb. If I am shaven, then my strength will leave me, and I shall become weak, and be like any other man.'
>
> "When Delilah saw that he had told her all his heart, she sent and called for the lords of the Philistines, saying, 'Come up once more, for he has told me all his heart.' So the lords of the Philistines came up to her and brought the money in their hand. Then she lulled him to sleep on her knees, and called for a man and had him shave off the seven locks of his head. Then she began to torment him, and his strength left him. And she said, 'The Philistines are upon you, Samson!' So he awoke from his sleep, and said, 'I will go out as before, at other times, and shake myself free!' But he did not know that the Lord had departed from him.
>
> "Then the Philistines took him and put out his eyes, and brought him down to Gaza. They bound him with bronze fetters, and he became a grinder in the prison" (Judges 16:4-21).

Samson's successes in life all came down to this. He had been successful as a judge over Israel: he had done physical exploits that would make today's Mixed Martial Arts (MMA) fighters look like helpless wimps. One relationship, a lustful infatuation with a Philistine girl, would seal his infamous fate. It could be argued that his encounter with Delilah was his eight seconds. His time of training, preparation, and dedication to the Lord had readied him for this. Would he ride successfully, or would he be quickly thrown off to be trampled under the feet of the Enemy? Although Samson did do many things right, the small things that seemed insignificant at the time would prove to be his eventual downfall.

When Samson got involved with Delilah, he was in a spiritual downturn that negated his previous preparation. Now, captured by the Philistines, Samson found himself forcefully blinded and working at a grinding mill with the slaves. I'm pretty sure he did some crisis praying as he walked around this grinding wheel day after day. Here was a man who had once been honored and highly respected, but now he had been reduced to a slave. He was the laughingstock of the entire ungodly Philistine nation.

This was a time of crisis prayer that should have never happened. It took Samson's pain and humiliation to bring him to a point of desperation that enabled him to personally connect with God again. Had he been spiritually in tune with God, the grinding mill would have never happened. As great as Samson's ministry was, as extensive as his legacy is, it could have, and should have been, even greater. Nevertheless, this is where the story actually takes a turn for the better. Just when you think the story is over, God steps in. God can step in and bring healing and transformation to anyone who will call upon Him in their time of need.

Even in the middle of all of Samson's bad decisions and indiscretions, the Bible points out something very interesting at the conclusion of this excerpt.

> "However, the hair of his head began to grow again after it had been shaven" (Judges 16:22).

This is incredibly powerful: Even after Samson forgot about God, God never forgot about Samson. As you read this story, maybe for the umpteenth time, know that God has never forgotten you either.

> "Be strong and of good courage, do not fear nor be afraid of them; for the *Lord* your God, He is the One who goes with you. He will not leave you nor forsake you" (Deuteronomy 31:6).

Samson once again found himself in a place of dire need for the Lord. In the past, shaking off chains and killing men with the jawbone of a donkey came easily. Not this time. Samson's shame was heavy and restrictive, but he cried out anyway. He asked the Lord to give him strength just one more time. God didn't turn a deaf ear, reminding Samson of his mistakes; instead a loving Father reached out and strengthened the errant strong man once more. Samson accomplished more at this death, by pushing the pillars of the temple and killing all who were inside, than he had during his life.

Even after Samson forgot about God, God never forgot about Samson.

Spiritual preparation isn't for the purpose of beating our chest and bragging about our high level of training. This type of preparation is for all believers so they can be at their very best and avoid unnecessary spiritual ups and downs. There's certainly always a time to pray about things, of course, but our spiritual preparation goes a long way to creating a successful life. If every single bump in the road sends you into a spiritual tail spin because you don't know what to do, you need to look much deeper at your preparation.

The apostle James reminds us that life is short, very short in fact. He gives us an illustration from the world of science as a visual reminder of how fleeting life actually is.

> "For what is your life? It is even a vapor that appears for a little time and then vanishes away" (James 4:14).

In the grand scheme of things, when compared to eternity, life is only a passing moment. As the cowboy prepares and trains for an eight-second stint on a wild bull, we must also prepare and train for the moments that count in our lives. Our lives are comprised of many eight-second experiences. These experiences, choices, and actions will define the legacy of our lives. For Ehud, his eight seconds took place in the private chamber of a wicked king. He was successful because he had prepared adequately for that encounter. Samson's final eight seconds ended in victory, despite his sin, because God loved him tirelessly. Make your eight seconds count because there are no do-overs.

Make your eight seconds count because there are no do-overs.

Chapter 5: Plot Twist

Chapter 5: Plot Twist

If you've ever watched a movie in which you could easily figure out the ending well before it actually ended, you probably thought to yourself, *This movie is boring and way too predictable*. The kind of movies that usually make it big are those that keep you guessing all the way up to the very end. Award-winning movies keep us glued to our seats and have us predicting any number of different scenarios as the finale. The famed plot twist is the goal of every writer; their desire is to keep people guessing incorrectly until the last minute.

Life can contain many plot twists. The things we plan on sometimes don't happen, and other things we don't anticipate end up happening anyway. Sometimes life just throws us a curveball that we could have never seen coming. Such was the case with Ehud, the warrior nobody ever saw coming.

A Left-Handed Man

The Bible doesn't tell us much about Ehud's life or even his own unique characteristics. However, the author does tell us something about Ehud that seems very strange to even mention: Ehud was a left-handed man.

> "But when the children of Israel cried out to the *Lord*, the *Lord* raised up a deliverer for them: Ehud the son of Gera, the Benjamite, a left-handed man…" (Judges 3:15).

Why would Scripture, which leaves out other seemingly important details, take the time to point out something that was so irrelevant? Why not tell us that he had blonde hair or that he was six feet tall? Why not tell us what kind of toothpaste or cereal he preferred? Why tell us such an obscure detail as this? Maybe this detail isn't so unimportant after all. Perhaps his dominant hand is the key to the entire assassination attempt.

It is estimated that in the world today only about 10% of the population is left-handed.[9] Why, with lefties being in the clear minority, did the author tell us this to underscore the quirkiness of Ehud? Were we supposed to realize that he had grown up feeling left out all of his life, or that he was somehow disenfranchised from all the people who were right-handed?

Consider this: Most every product is designed for right-handed people. Not because they are loved more, but simply because they are the overwhelming majority, and majority rules! In the times of the Judges, this would have also been the case. The world was designed (especially at that time in history) for the right-handed. Warriors were trained to fight right-handed. Weaponry was designed for right-handed personnel, and hand-to-hand combat training was designed with the right-handed in mind. As a warrior, Ehud was a left-handed man in a right-handed world.

Some consider being left-handed a handicap, of sorts. In fact, Scripture only mentions people being left-handed a handful of times, and in every instance, the left-handed person is from the tribe of Benjamin. Why is that important? Benjamin was the youngest son of Jacob, and became the father of the twelfth tribe of Israel. In Hebrew culture, the oldest son got a double portion for an inheritance, whereas the other sons received a single portion. There seems to be almost an established pecking order: Each new son was viewed as slightly less honored than his older counterparts.

God Uses the Least Qualified

In the Bible, people claim to be the *"least in their father's household."* Such was the case with David, Gideon, Benjamin, and others. People coming from the tribe of Benjamin, although all tribes were in some way blessed by the Lord, seemed to have a little bit of an uphill battle, simply

9. Kate Bratskeir, "11 Little-Known Facts About Left-Handers," The Huffington Post, October 29, 2012, accessed October 05, 2017, http://www.huffingtonpost.com/2012/10/29/left-handed-facts-lefties_n_2005864.html.

because of the tribal pecking order. Ehud, although we're not sure of his particular birth order, was a Benjamite. His being both a Benjamite and a leftie makes him seem somewhat unlikely as a standout warrior, who would be hand-selected for a supremely covert assassination mission.

It is very interesting that people we may deem as unqualified or as not having the right tools for the job are the very people that God chooses to use. The scriptural list of "misfit toys," so to speak, is long. Moses was a stutterer and a murderer when God called him to lead the nation of Israel out of Egyptian bondage. King David was only a shepherd and had absolutely no political experience at all when God ordained him to lead the nation. When we first meet Gideon, he was threshing wheat in a winepress in order to hide the grain from the Midianites. He was hiding from the very opposition that God was equipping him to attack.

People we may deem as unqualified or as not having the right tools for the job are the very people that God chooses to use.

Ehud was such a man too. He had no known history as an assassin, a covert operation leader, and as far as we know, he wasn't even known for his impressive fighting skills. Yet, God, who could have chosen and equipped anyone on the earth for this incredible, faith-filled venture, chose a left-handed Benjamite by the name of Ehud. Is there a specific reason in this passage that his dominant hand is mentioned? I would submit to you that what other people may have considered a weakness, God was specifically looking to use.

The Undetected Weapon

We know from studying history and seeing pictures of ancient warriors, that the uniform, armor, and weaponry were all critical in terms of their look as well as their placement. When you look at artists' renderings of old battle scenes, the warriors look almost like superheroes. The men are usually covered in sweat and blood; their armor looks like it might weigh hundreds of pounds; and their swords and shields are massive pieces of handcrafted metal, designed to stop even the most intense attack. They're a far cry from the computer-generated war plans of today, with heat-seeking missiles and GPS-guided bombs. Ancient warriors relied solely upon brute strength and sheer determination.

Warriors spent weeks on end camping in the battlefield, many times with few if any of the comforts of home, and with limited food and water supplies. The small details that would offer even the slightest comfort were highly important. The comfort of their helmets, the fit of their chest piece, all the way down to the comfort of their boots, could make the difference between a successful battle and one that ended in death. In addition to comfort, the practical aspects of battlefield warfare also had to be considered.

Ancient warriors carried nothing into battle other than that which was absolutely necessary. Personal keepsakes, creature comforts, or anything else that added weight to the warrior was shed in order to be as lean and quick as possible. This was minimalism at its best; only the necessary items were taken into battle. Commanding officers often ran through a checklist with their men to ensure they were carrying the essentials, but nothing more.

Another consideration in battle beyond the quantity of gear, was the actual placement of their weapons. When faced with a life-threatening confrontation, a man couldn't waste any time searching for the weapon of choice. Even a few seconds of frantic patting, looking for a knife, a dagger, or a blunt object could mean the difference between living to fight another day, and dying a bloody death on the battlefield.

The sword was one of these carefully-placed weapons on the side of every warrior. In most depictions of ancient warriors, you will see either a sword in his hand or a sword sheathed on his side. The sword was, without a doubt, the weapon of choice for every person on the battlefield. The sword provided a reach advantage over simple hand-to-hand combat; it offered the possibility of quick and precise death; and it could be easily sheathed for quick movement following a confrontation.

Swords are mentioned frequently in historic writings, including the Bible, and were, without question, the most significant weapon for battle.

Ehud was faced with an enormous challenge. He needed to get into King Eglon's private chamber with an undetected weapon. How was this possible? Prior to entry, he would be searched by the king's personal security team. This was an all-or-nothing proposition; if he was caught, he died. If he fumbled in any way, was seen by security with a weapon, or didn't get the private meeting, this wouldn't be a hero's story, but a tribute to a foiled attempt.

We know that Ehud had audience with the king, as he was there to carry the annual tribute from the people of Israel. The meeting was set, the time confirmed, Ehud had the money, and now all the pieces had to fit just right for this to succeed. But how do you smuggle a weapon past security without detection? Well, it becomes a little easier if you're left-handed.

Knowing that such a small percentage of people were actually left-handed meant that security probably would not expect a lefty. Since he was left-handed, Ehud strapped his dagger, which is a shorter version of a sword, onto his right side. This made for a quick draw in a confrontation. Think about it. If you drew your sword from the dominant side, it would be tricky to pull it up high enough and turn it quickly enough to use it. For both comfort and maneuverability, the sword was most often strapped to the side that wasn't dominant. Reaching across the body to pull the sword afforded extra room for the sword to be properly positioned for engagement. A right-handed warrior strapped his weapon on the left side, and Ehud, being left-handed, strapped his dagger to his right side and concealed it, placing it under his clothes.

> "Now Ehud made himself a dagger (it was double-edged and a cubit in length) and fastened it under his clothes on his right thigh" (Judges 3:16).

Ehud walked into the king's courts carrying the tribute money and was subject to a search by the king's personal security guards. The Bible doesn't provide a lot of detail here regarding exactly how this happened, but I can't imagine these men allowing a foreigner to come in bringing tribute to the king without a thorough search. The search began by simply looking at Ehud, what he wore, how he walked, the look on his face, and his body language. Ehud had to be careful not to act suspicious or give even a hint of his true purpose.

These men were the only thing standing between an assassination attempt and their king. This job was not to be taken lightly; and in most ancient cultures, failure at this level was punished by execution. Make no mistake about it: These men weren't a bunch of preoccupied teenagers! They were highly trained specialists. They weren't given the option to make excuses for mismanaged screening. The life of the king depended upon their success all the time, every time.

Security most likely asked him if he had any weapons to which he would have responded, "No." Then the physical search began, most likely a pat down, and a more intense visual search. Keep in mind: The warriors that the Moabites were used to dealing with, including their own warriors, were right-handed men. The concentration for the search would, without question, focus on the warrior's left side. A right-handed man would never carry weaponry on his right side and Ehud's specially crafted dagger was easily overlooked by the security detail. After the pat down revealed nothing, Ehud was free to enter the king's private chamber to deliver Israel's tribute.

Did you get that? Since Ehud was left-handed, some commanders would have argued that he was not even fit for battle. He was in the overwhelming minority of all the people, and certainly in the minority of military men. When choosing a single warrior to undertake a task of this magnitude, Ehud wouldn't have been their first choice. In fact, he would probably have likely been their last. But this task wasn't like any other. This wasn't an assignment designed and crafted by military geniuses sitting around a planning table. This was a specific mission created by God Himself.

God looks at things completely differently than man. Man is prone to look at things through the lens of personal weakness, while God looks at possibilities from the vantage point of His own strength. Not only was a left-handed warrior a potential candidate, he was exactly what God was looking for in this specific assignment.

God Wants Our Availability

The Devil has this unique ability to make us feel as if we are somehow not able to do the things God has empowered us to do. As God begins to speak to us about doing something significant, the first thing that usually happens is that our minds begin to be flooded with doubts about our own capabilities. What Satan knows, and we tend to forget, is that a person fully submitted to God has unlimited possibilities. The famous evangelist D.L. Moody once said, "The world has yet to see what God can do with a man fully consecrated to Him. By God's help, I aim to be that man."[10]

What Satan knows, and we tend to forget, is that a person fully submitted to God has unlimited possibilities.

The Enemy fears the person who realizes that God doesn't need our ability. God is simply looking for availability. When the left-handed warrior walked into the king's courts to carry out one of the greatest assassination attempts in history, it must have been humbling to realize that he had been born for this exact moment. The Bible tells us that God raised up a deliverer for Israel. Before Ehud was ever born, the destiny of God was written all over his life. He may have had a wife, a family, or an additional career besides being a soldier, but he was designed to be successful at this moment. Of course, there were other successful moments that would come, but at this time, nothing was more pressing than Ehud's success. The nation needed a man submitted to God; they needed a man with skill, bravery, and opportunity. The nation needed a left-handed warrior!

10. Mark Fackler, "The World Has Yet to See...," Christian History | Learn the History of Christianity & the Church, 1990, accessed October 06, 2017, http://www.christianitytoday.com/history/issues/issue-25/world-has-yet-to-see.html.

How many times have we made pathetic excuses about our lack of action for the Lord? It is easy to dismiss God's urging as some crazy idea or some misguided attempt to be a visionary. What if you had the ability to do absolutely anything for the Lord? The sky's the limit. If there was nothing stopping you: money, skill, connections, or anything else, what would you do? Does that question scare you a bit? If it does, that may be because that's a God-sized dream that only He could make happen. Before the assassination of Eglon, the left-handed warrior was just a common warrior. Of course, he despised the persecution and bondage of his people, but what was he supposed to do?

This question strikes at the very heart of our faith and personal validation. It's easy for me to believe God can use someone else, but when it comes to Him actually using *me*, that's a bit different. Can you imagine what was running through Ehud's head when he began to feel God speaking to him regarding the assassination of King Eglon? I'm sure the excuses began to flow and sounded something like this: *God, I've never done anything like this before. Surely someone else is more qualified. I have no experience, no plan, no backup, and besides, I'm left-handed.* To which God would have simply replied, "I know; that's why I chose you."

Our Weakness: His Strength

Realize this: God already knows your résumé. God is familiar with your strengths and weaknesses, as well as your potential for success. Arguing with God about your potential is like arguing with your mother about why you should be required to make your bed. You can argue as much as you want, but in the end, she always wins. This is the point: God doesn't need us, we need Him. Anything that I have the privilege to accomplish for the Lord is because I was fortunate enough to have been used by Him.

The plot twist of your life will occur when God takes what looks like your handicap, and uses it for His purposes to show His strength. When Ehud walked into the king's courts, the expectation was that he would just hand over the tribute, like he had all the years before. The plot twist was that God stepped into what should have been ordinary and made it extraordinary. Ehud was the one nobody saw coming. You are the thing that nobody ever saw coming too. God wants to use you far beyond anything you or anyone else has ever imagined.

The plot twist of your life will occur when God takes what looks like your handicap, and uses it for His purposes to show His strength.

Who else but the Lord could take a young boy by the name of Joseph, hated by his brothers and sold into slavery, and promote him to VP status in a foreign country? Who else could take a rebellious prophet, thrown overboard by his crew to have him swallowed by a large fish and spit up on dry land, to be used once again by God? Who but the Lord could take a young shepherd boy with no battle experience and use him to defeat a nine-foot giant? I'm telling you, God can use anybody to do anything if they are fully yielded to Him.

God Thinks about You

I believe that Satan begins to shake in his boots when God's people begin to get even an inkling of what God's plans are for their lives. We serve an unlimited God with unlimited thoughts and potential for people who sadly are quick to put limitations on themselves. God's Word is very clear about how He thinks about us.

> "For I know the thoughts that I think toward you, says the *Lord*, thoughts of peace and not of evil, to give you a future and a hope" (Jeremiah 29:11).

This verse has such deep meaning. Everyone needs to have this memorized. When our kids were small, we made them learn this verse. To this day, each one of them has this Scripture tattooed on their brains. We want them to know that regardless of how things may look, God has plans for them that are bigger than anything they could ever imagine.

Jeremiah the prophet wrote this verse as part of a letter addressed to the Jewish exiles in Babylon. Many of the people had become so discouraged and bitter over their surroundings that they had basically given up on ever having a nation or any semblance of national pride. The Hebrew people had been overthrown by the Babylonian Empire, and now many of the people were held hostage in Babylon against their will. They longed to go home, they longed to worship, they longed for freedom. These things that were previously taken for granted now seemed a million miles away and likely to never be seen again in their lifetime.

When the people were at their lowest, God began to speak to Jeremiah to bring encouragement and perspective to the people. They were not forgotten, they were not abandoned, they were not all alone; God was still with them. In Jeremiah 29:11, God reminded the people of these things. He told them that He "thought" about them. That is such a humbling statement. Think about that—God thinks about you. What does He think? He tells us! He says, "thoughts of peace and not of evil." This is the antithesis of what Satan thinks towards us. Satan wants us to be destroyed, he wants our hope to be gone, and he wants our future to be forgotten.

> "Be sober, be vigilant; because your adversary the devil walks about like a roaring lion, seeking whom he may devour" (1 Peter 5:8).

As God begins to stir you for action, your impossible destiny, your moment with the Moabite king, know that there are two completely opposing views which will confront you. I'm sure you have seen the old picture of a person put in the awkward position of trying to do the right thing. On one shoulder, a harp-playing angel gives the person good advice that will render good results. On the other shoulder, a pitchfork-wielding devil in a red suit speaks the opposite, attempting to dissuade the decision maker. Although this is not exactly how it works, it does have a ring of truth.

Ehud had every reason in the world not to go through with his plan: to fail would mean humiliation followed by execution. When God begins to stir you, Satan will begin to distract you. God says, "You can" and

Satan says, "You can't." God says, "I've formed you for this purpose." Satan says, "Anyone could do a better job than you. Don't even try." We must tune our hearts to listen to the voice of God, and surrender our plans to His. Truth be told, God's plan fulfilled in your life could be the next big plot twist.

When God begins to stir you, Satan will begin to distract you.

Making Excuses

Moses was also a man used by God to do something much bigger than he could have ever imagined. When God first began to speak to Moses, we find him full of excuses and multiple reasons as to why someone else should do what God needed done. The people of Israel were enslaved by the Egyptians and living through a terrible time in their history. Moses, who was a Hebrew by blood, in a strange turn of God-ordained events wound up being raised by the Pharaoh's daughter.

He saw the horrors of his people's bondage, and decided he could no longer live in denial. When he withstood an Egyptian, who was beating a Hebrew slave, the fight escalated and ended in a dead Egyptian. Afraid to be charged with murder, Moses fled to the desert and chose to live what he thought would be the remainder of his life in hiding. God, however, had different plans. He began to speak to Moses about his role in leading the people to a land of promise and out of bondage.

> "And the Angel of the Lord appeared to him in a flame of fire from the midst of a bush. So he looked, and behold, the bush was burning with fire, but the bush was not consumed. Then Moses said, 'I will now turn aside and see this great sight, why the bush does not burn.'

> "So when the Lord saw that he turned aside to look, God called to him from the midst of the bush and said, 'Moses, Moses!' And he said, 'Here I am.'
>
> "Then He said, 'Do not draw near this place. Take your sandals off your feet, for the place where you stand is holy ground.' Moreover He said, 'I am the God of your father—the God of Abraham, the God of Isaac, and the God of Jacob.' And Moses hid his face, for he was afraid to look upon God.
>
> "And the Lord said: 'I have surely seen the oppression of My people who are in Egypt, and have heard their cry because of their taskmasters, for I know their sorrows. So I have come down to deliver them out of the hand of the Egyptians, and to bring them up from that land to a good and large land, to a land flowing with milk and honey, to the place of the Canaanites and the Hittites and the Amorites and the Perizzites and the Hivites and the Jebusites. Now therefore, behold, the cry of the children of Israel has come to Me, and I have also seen the oppression with which the Egyptians oppress them. Come now, therefore, and I will send you to Pharaoh that you may bring My people, the children of Israel, out of Egypt'" (Exodus 3:2-10).

This is an incredible opportunity, the opportunity for which Moses was born. God shows Himself to Moses in a way that was unmistakable, and speaks to him in an audible voice. Moses has the assurance of God's call and success, yet Moses did what most of us do in this same scenario. We tend to disguise our fear with excuses. Moses gave no less than five reasons as to why he couldn't or shouldn't be the person to lead God's people.

Reason #1: I am not the right person for the job!

> "But Moses said to God, 'Who am I that I should go to Pharaoh, and that I should bring the children of Israel out of Egypt?'" (Exodus 3:11).

God wasn't looking for a person who was good enough. He was looking for a person who was willing to obey the call. As God begins to direct us, our insecurities and reasons why we are not being qualified will quickly rise to the surface

Reason #2: I don't even know what to say!

> "Then Moses said to God, 'Indeed, when I come to the children of Israel and say to them, "The God of your fathers has sent me to you," and they say to me, "What is His name?" what shall I say to them?'" (Exodus 3:13).

Did Moses actually think that God was going to hang him out to dry? Why would God give him a clear mission, authority, and the wisdom to carry out that mission, and then overlook a detail as small as the proper words needed to communicate well? God is much bigger than we have the capacity to understand. At the time of this meeting between Moses and God, Moses had no idea of the magnitude of miracles that would happen through his hands.

Reason #3: I have zero credibility!

> "Then Moses answered and said, 'But suppose they will not believe me or listen to my voice; suppose they say, "The *Lord* has not appeared to you."'" (Exodus 4:1).

This is every salesman or public speaker's worst fear: an audience with which they cannot connect. Moses was saying, "They will call me a liar!" God's response was to ask Moses what he was holding in his hand. This was God's way of showing Moses that He would never leave him holding the bag all by himself. Moses threw down his shepherd's staff and it instantly became a dangerous snake. God told him to pick it up; Moses reluctantly obeyed and God turned the snake back into a shepherd's staff. This should have been enough, an open-and-shut case, but Moses wasn't done yet.

Reason # 4: I can't put two complete sentences together!

> "Then Moses said to the *Lord*, 'O my Lord, I am not eloquent, neither before nor since You have spoken to Your servant; but I am slow of speech and slow of tongue'" (Exodus 4:10).

And we're back again. Moses own insecurities are causing him to grasp at straws. God has just turned a rod into a snake and then back again, and here's Moses carrying on about his word choices. When we hear his reasoning from the vantage point of looking backwards, this seems so petty. Hindsight is 20/20. When you're in the story, however, the excuses seem completely valid. After Moses seemingly covered every area of possible excuses, he manages to find one more.

Reason #5: You've got the wrong guy!

> But he said, "O my Lord, please send by the hand of whomever else You may send" (Exodus 4:13).

We cannot expect to make any real progress forward while simultaneously making excuses.

Notice that reason number five and reason number one are essentially the same. This is what avoiding the plan of God does in our lives: It leads us in endless circles. We cannot expect to make any real progress forward while simultaneously making excuses. This is one of the Devil's most successful plans. While you may think you are simply gaining clarity, you are actually spinning your wheels and going nowhere. With all that the Lord shared with Moses, it makes no sense at all that God had the wrong person.

God's call on our life is no mistake. All Moses saw was his own personal weaknesses and inabilities. All God saw was a man who had been uniquely prepared for this specific mission. When God puts His hand on our shoulders and moves us to greater purpose, He will never put us in a position to retreat and watch us fail. He is faithful to stand with us along the way and make our venture successful. As the Lord spoke through Jeremiah to the discouraged nation, God is speaking to us today. He plans for us to prosper, He plans for us to succeed, and He plans for us to embrace and fulfill the future designed for us.

When God puts His hand on our shoulders and moves us to greater purpose, He will never put us in a position to retreat and watch us fail.

As this chapter concludes, I want to encourage you to allow the Lord, the Author of our lives, to complete the story of your life. Our story is seldom predictable and seldom linear. It has many curves and bumps. One thing I do know: God is not a starter only, He is a finisher. He doesn't abandon His projects midstream, nor does He lose interest along the way. God has had your life planned from before you were born, and His plan still remains.

> "looking unto Jesus, the author and finisher of our faith, who for the joy that was set before Him endured the cross, despising the shame, and has sat down at the right hand of the throne of God" (Hebrews 12:2).

We can choose to live our lives in a way that is bound by society, attempting to make everyone happy. We can choose to live in bondage to the expectations of family, friends, or even our own ideas of what "successful" looks like. We can also choose to live in complete obedience to God and follow His direction and will for our lives. These different descriptions may not always describe the same path. Sometimes they are completely different. Man's path and God's path seldom look the same.

In fact, they are usually much different. Ehud's path was probably pretty much set: Just live as a faithful man of God. Don't cause any trouble and eventually God will set us free. Thankfully, Ehud wasn't satisfied with a preselected path. He was open and obedient to God's higher plan. Ehud's path wasn't linear; it surely wasn't easy and without stress; and it contained a plot twist that nobody saw coming. Today, let God be the Author of your life, plot twists and all, and just watch what He can do!

Chapter 6:
Lionhearted

Chapter 6: Lionhearted

The lion is universally known as the king of the jungle. Sitting at the top of the food chain, lions are known as apex predators.[11] An apex predator is an animal with no known predator within its ecosystem. They are sometimes beautiful, but not normally considered the friendly house pet variety of animal.

I had the privilege of traveling to Botswana in Africa to visit a Bible school and preach in some local churches a few years ago. While I was there, a group of guys decided to take a trip just south of the Botswanan border to neighboring South Africa, in order to visit a wild game reserve. We were going to be able to see what they call the big five. The big five are the following: rhinoceros, elephant, Cape buffalo, leopard and lion.

This was definitely on my bucket list. From childhood, I remembered watching the old animal documentaries and seeing the wild animals of the African plain. I remember seeing the big crocodiles eating small animals, baby birds hatching and being fed, hummingbirds hovering over flowers, but nothing got my blood pumping like a good lion chase. To see the lion hiding in the grass, slowly making its selection of an animal he wanted on the menu, and stealthily creeping up, flattened nearly to the ground was heart stopping.

As we began to travel around the reserve on a large ATV we saw many different animals. We saw beautifully colored birds, gazelles,

11. Todd Smith, "The 10 Most Deadly Apex Predators on Earth," Sportsman Channel, November 29, 2016, accessed October 06, 2017, http://www.thesportsmanchannel.com/2015/04/10-deadly-apex-predators-earth.

wildebeests, and even giraffes. Since I had only seen these animals before on television, they were all incredibly fascinating. I snapped picture after picture with my phone so I could share what I saw with my family. My boys were particularly interested in the wildlife of Africa, and I knew they would be most interested in the monkeys and lions.

Although I was having the time of my life, and grateful for the experience, I was anxious to see what I really came to see. The beauty of the African plain was breathtaking, but what I really wanted to see was the famed African lion. The trip we were on began in the evening of one day, and we slept and woke early in the morning for our second phase of the safari. I couldn't help but wonder: *Are we going to be able to see a lion today?* Well, I didn't have to wonder about that for very long.

Our vehicle pulled up to a particular area that was fenced off for the safety of the visitors. Lined up along this fence were warning signs that were very explicit about not putting your hands through the fence, watching small children, and so on. This was the viewing area for the lions; I couldn't have been more excited.

Our safari guide went to a cooler where he had some meat stored for this very purpose. He began to yell and whistle loudly as he threw the meat over the fence; it was feeding time for the lions. Out in the distance in a wooded area, there quickly began to be some movement. Sure enough, ten to twelve lions came running toward us for their morning feeding.

This wasn't exactly the lion chase I had envisioned, but it was still an amazing sight. These lions began to feed viciously on the meat given them. It looked like rib portions, and the lions made quick work of it. I can distinctly remember the sound of those bones being crushed by their powerful jaws. The sound of crunching bones was so loud that everyone in the group began commenting about it.

I thought to myself, *No wonder this is the king of the beasts with jaws this strong!* The lion has nothing to fear. These strong, muscular animals practically inhaled their allotted food. The ones that ate more quickly than the others turned and tried to take what was left from some of the smaller lions. It was clear that there was a hierarchy of respect, and the smaller lions quickly gave up what was left of their food in order to avoid an ugly fight.

Fearing Failure

The lion has become synonymous with the word "bravery" simply because the lion really has very little to fear. Such is the child of God when we begin to realize how strong we actually are. As the lion has been equipped with speed, agility, and strength, the child of God has also been equipped for great success.

Ehud was a man of incredible bravery. It's interesting to me that sometimes we quickly read through stories like this without really taking the time to think about what the surrounding circumstances must have been like. Ehud wasn't a modern-day vigilante or bounty hunter like we see depicted in action movies. He was just a man who had a desire to be used by God. Regardless of how perfect the plan may have been, the key ingredient for all of this to happen successfully was that little seven letter word: bravery.

For Ehud, this wasn't a trial and error situation, like launching a new business. This had much higher stakes. Success would make him a national hero with a legacy that would endure throughout history. Failure would bring him certain death and immeasurable pain to the Hebrew people as a whole.

Sometimes you have to reach down deep inside yourself and find your bravery.

It's easy to read this and think, *Ehud knew God was on his side. He had to succeed.* That's easy to say, but hard to live. We are reading this story from start to finish, whereas Ehud was seeing things through the perspective of real time. In the middle of your struggles, it's easy to quote the clichés and the power scriptures, but the bottom line is this: Sometimes you have to reach down deep inside yourself and find your bravery.

What if I fail? is a common thought we all face at some point in our lives. Can you imagine what a boring world this would be if nobody had the bravery to risk failure? There would never be any new businesses, as new businesses have a fairly high failure rate. There would be no new churches, because churches have the capacity to fail also. What about stepping out on a limb to get married? Marriages are subject to separation, painful circumstances, and even worse; divorce. There would be no new technological or medical breakthroughs, and the list goes on. The possibility of failure will always exist. That's the bottom line.

When God speaks to us and begins to give us direction and purpose for our lives, Satan has to combat that, or risk suffering personal defeat. Satan will never stand back and let you win the world for Christ and decrease the size of hell without opposition. The power of God is within you, and Satan knows that he is no match.

> "You are of God, little children, and have overcome them, because He who is in you is greater than he who is in the world" (1 John 4:4).

Satan can't actually outmatch you, but that doesn't stop him from trying to get you to self-destruct. Fear is his bread and butter. As God begins to give you a glimpse of the future, the Enemy immediately floods your mind with anxiety, doubt, and fear. I'm sure when you read the great exploits in the Bible, you realize that these accomplishments weren't done without fear. When Daniel took a stand before being thrown in the lion's den, I'm pretty confident he had a certain level of fear. The difference between the lionhearted and the missed opportunity is how we deal with fear.

The question we must answer is: "Did God speak to me and give me direction about this?" If the answer to that question is yes, then we know we will succeed. I realize that fear isn't like a light switch that we can simply turn off. However, daily prayer and reading God's Word brings about confidence in the Lord that allows us to shake off what the Enemy tries to get us to own. Nobody wants to fail; everyone wants to succeed. Satan will sometimes bring up your past failures as evidence that your future is destined for failure as well.

> Satan can't actually outmatch you, but that doesn't stop him from trying to get you to self-destruct.

Satan is a specialist in diversion techniques too. Many movies depict the mastermind scheme of criminals robbing a bank. Smart people don't just go into the bank with guns blazing. They create a diversion instead, so they can get in and out without anyone noticing them. Perhaps pulling a fire alarm box a few blocks away, or starting a public disturbance of some sort away from the actual robbery location will help. Why would they do this? The idea is that law enforcement would be focused on the wrong place and the wrong set of circumstances while criminals executed their plan in secret. The genius of the diversion is that people can't be in more than one place at a time.

The Enemy doesn't want us to be focused on God's plan. He knows that with all of God's resources, in addition to our strong dedication, he is no competition. Satan loves roadblocks, speed bumps, and false alarms. When we are sidetracked by our past discouragements, this is a clear indication that Satan has created a diversion. When we are afraid we might fail and it keeps us from moving forward, this is also a diversion. There is no way I can be focused on God's plan for my life and be distracted by the Enemy at the same time.

Don't let the fear of failure or even the reality of a bad experience keep you from being the person that God has empowered you to be. Fear is one of the surefire tactics of Satan that can prevent you from reaching your potential.

Overcoming Fear

> "For God has not given us a spirit of fear, but of power and of love and of a sound mind" (2 Timothy 1:7).

If you are experiencing fear, know that this is not of God. God does not motivate or direct the course of our lives with fear. Was Ehud feeling some anxiety before his assassination attempt? I'm sure he was, but fear is something altogether different. Fear is paralyzing; it is debilitating; it keeps you so emotional that you would rather do nothing than do something. 2 Timothy tells us that God invests the complete antithesis of fear in us. God gives us three things to counteract and overcome fear.

Power

God gives us power. The words used here comes from the Greek *dunamis* and it means "miraculous power; ability, abundance, might, violent strength."[12] Both "dynamite" and "dynamo" come from this word. This isn't just a little firecracker tossed on the sidewalk kind of power either. This isn't small or insignificant. This is Devil-chasing, mountain moving, make-the-Devil-regret-ever-bothering-with-you kind of power.

This is the kind of power that allowed Jesus to make a bold statement regarding the faith of the believer.

> "For assuredly, I say to you, whoever says to this mountain, 'Be removed and be cast into the sea,' and does not doubt in his heart, but believes that those things he says will be done, he will have whatever he says" (Mark 11:23).

This is power! When you look at this verse in its context, the mountain Jesus is talking about is the mountain of adversity (or difficulty) in our lives. It means that regardless of what you face or the size of what you face, God is bigger. We've all had mountains: mountains of pain, debt, discouragement, confusion, and more. Know this: Every mountain is

---

12. James Strong, Strong's exhaustive concordance of the Bible (New York: Abingdon Press, 1890).

subject to God's amazing power. Some mountains are just waiting for the right person to speak to them.

When Ehud stood before King Eglon, he may not have stood as a man with an impressive résumé, but he did stand as man with mountain-moving faith and the heart of a lion. His faith had to come from something much deeper than his own experience or his past victories. Ehud carried the power in Him that came not only from a man on a mission, but from a man who knew the power of his God. You might be thinking, *That sounds great, but that's a Bible story. This man was full of faith, but I'm no Ehud.* But that's not true. You are an Ehud too, because Ehud was a regular person, just like you and me! We aren't superheroes, and most likely never will be. We don't have the ability to somehow be removed from life's problems. The day-to-day routines in our world can sometimes be taxing and hard to deal with. This is the same world that Ehud lived in. He wasn't immune to problems or the reality of his decisions either. He simply had a deep trust in God and realized that God was on his side.

There have been times in my life when what I was feeling was anything but power. I'm sure you have had the same. God has a way of placing the right thing in our life at the right time to show us that He is, in fact, in control and will cause us to succeed. For Ehud, there were a number of open doors along the way. He got past the guards, he had access to the king, and he was able to have a private meeting. The doors seemed to continually open to allow him to fulfill his plan. When God is at work in your life, there is a source of power that goes beyond anything you can do on your own. His power is so overwhelmingly complete that He leaves nothing undone, and I mean nothing. Ehud didn't have to die a martyr either. God protected him with a way of escape and gave him long life, even after his gutsy move.

Love

The power that God gives us is a major tool in our arsenal, but He also gives us love. This word comes from the Greek *agapé*[13] and refers to

13. Ibid.

God's unconditional love.[14] This means God loves us before, during, and after failure. God cannot love you any more than He already does! It goes a long way to know that God loves me and has my back, no matter how many mistakes I make. His love is so complete that it is not circumstantial, meaning that His love is not conditional and not based upon your current circumstances. When you're good, He loves you; when you're not so good, you guessed it, He still loves you. Fear of rejection by God or fear that He somehow may disapprove so strongly that He gives up on us is completely inaccurate. What if Ehud would have blown his cover? What if he would have been so afraid he gave himself away while talking to the king? He could have bumbled the assassination attempt and put his entire country at risk. If that had happened, God would have still loved him. Don't let fear of rejection keep you from being what God has already accepted; God loves you and that is final!

Don't let fear of rejection keep you from being what God has already accepted

The love of God is hard to understand, but if you're a parent you have had the joy of seeing a precious little one born in to the world. I remember when my daughter was born; she was our firstborn child. My wife and I were very young, and we were full of questions and anxiety about being responsible for another human life. The moment she was born, we had an intense feeling of love for this little girl. She wasn't even a minute old, but I knew we would have a special relationship. The bond between a parent and a child, though powerful, is still only a shadow of the love God has for us.

When you really walk in the truth that the God of this universe actually loves you, it gives you permission to overlook many things. When I realize that He loves me, somehow what other people may say or think about me really doesn't matter nearly as much. Because His love is so much stronger than fear, in times of worry I run to Him. It is amazing!

14. Ibid.

When I'm fearful of the future or concerned about a decision I'm making, I go to Him and find myself immersed in His love. At the end of the day, when you realize that God is absolutely in love with you, your fears are reduced to minor inconveniences.

Sound Mind

Finally, as the antithesis of fear, God gives us a sound mind. That's pretty encouraging, as sometimes I question that about myself! This phrase comes from the Greek *sophronismos* which means "discipline, self-control, not prone to extremes."[15] Therefore, God is saying that through prayer and hearing His voice, we will not go far off course. Sometimes God will allow us to venture out a little bit and experience the correction necessary to keep us focused; but by being attentive, we won't stray far. The sound mind is the mind of Christ that Paul speaks about.

> "Let this mind be in you which was also in Christ Jesus" (Philippians 2:5).

Ehud probably questioned his state of mind many times as he played and replayed this life-or-death decision. The life of faith will always cause us to stand on what may appear to be an unsteady foundation. However, God always proves Himself completely faithful to us. The mind of Christ cannot be broken or even swayed by fear. The mind of Christ is one that has full confidence in the Word of God, and full confidence that if we err, He'll be there to pick us up, dust us off, and believe in us yet again.

The mind is the point of access for fear. Most of the things we fear never actually happen. We have the tendency to think in terms of the "worst case scenario." Not that bad things can't happen, but the majority of our fears never come to pass. We are masters of the "what if": What if this happens or what if that happens? Try changing your way of thinking to sound more like: *What if God is faithful to do what He said? What if I am obedient to Him and allow Him to use me?*

---

15. Ibid.

I have no doubt that Ehud had to consider what could happen, but the bravery within him was able to reign in that fear, and say, "I will be successful." There was no time for fear, there was no time to say, "What if?" There was only time to draw on his bravery, be lionhearted, and do what he was born to do.

The battle against fear starts and finishes in the mind.

The battle against fear starts and finishes in the mind. When we decide to follow Jesus, it doesn't just mean we go to church and stop carousing with sinners. It means we are changed by God. We are inhabited by the Spirit of God and changed within. Coupled with this, there is a transformation in our mind.

> "And do not be conformed to this world, but be transformed by the renewing of your mind, that you may prove what is that good and acceptable and perfect will of God" (Romans 12:2).

The world has a worldly mind, and thus thinks worldly thoughts. The believer, however, has a mind that has been purchased by the blood of Jesus and is in the process of an ongoing transformation. Think about the fear in the world right now. There is the fear of dying, getting diseases, running out of money, war, violence, and the list goes on forever. For the believer, those things are worth mental consideration, but we don't have to get consumed with any of those issues. The reason: God is in ultimate control and He has the final say in everything and we trust Him!

He Is Our Confidence

Being lionhearted doesn't mean having a big roar or bone-crushing jaws. It's not about being an apex predator either. It's about having overwhelming confidence in the Lord. Mark 5 tells a story about a lionhearted woman in need of relief, relief that could only come from the Lord.

> "Now a certain woman had a flow of blood for twelve years, and had suffered many things from many physicians. She had spent all that she had and was no better, but rather grew worse. When she heard about Jesus, she came behind Him in the crowd and touched His garment. For she said, 'If only I may touch His clothes, I shall be made well.'
>
> "Immediately the fountain of her blood was dried up, and she felt in her body that she was healed of the affliction. And Jesus, immediately knowing in Himself that power had gone out of Him, turned around in the crowd and said, 'Who touched My clothes?'
>
> "But His disciples said to Him, 'You see the multitude thronging You, and You say, 'Who touched Me?'
>
> "And He looked around to see her who had done this thing. But the woman, fearing and trembling, knowing what had happened to her, came and fell down before Him and told Him the whole truth. And He said to her, 'Daughter, your faith has made you well. Go in peace, and be healed of your affliction'" (Mark 5:25-34).

This woman had a constant menstrual condition for twelve years! Twelve years of suffering, and twelve years of visiting doctors. Medicine in her day was trial and error at best, and this caused her great pain and a lot of money. In fact, she had spent everything she had in trying to find a cure; and instead of making progress, she actually became worse.

Day in and day out, she searched for a cure. She went to doctor after doctor, many physicians getting her hopes up, promising to help only to have her spirit crushed, as she realized her condition had only worsened. She had to experience deep disappointment and frustration as everything she tried ended in yet another letdown. This wasn't a condition she dealt with for a short period of time, but a very long time. Twelve years is three presidential terms, it's more than a decade, it's the age a kid enters the sixth grade. This wasn't a minor inconvenience, this was something that consumed her life, as she desperately searched for relief.

You have to realize that her pain was much deeper than just the physical discomfort; there were other implications as well. According to Mosaic Law, a woman on her menstrual cycle was considered unclean and was forbidden the opportunity to participate in regular religious worship.

> "'Thus you shall separate the children of Israel from their uncleanness, lest they die in their uncleanness when they defile My tabernacle that is among them'" (Leviticus 15:31).

Anyone she touched, anything she sat or lay upon was considered to be unclean. She wasn't even allowed into the temple for customary times of prayer and worship. It's one thing to have to miss church because you have the flu, but what must it have been like to endure twelve years of sickness with no end in sight? This woman was suffering physically as a result of her own sickness and failed medical procedures too. She was suffering financially because she spent all her money searching for a cure. Additionally, she was suffering spiritually because of her inability to enter into worship with the rest of her people. And who knows what other ill effects this illness brought into her life and into her relationships! It must have been awful.

She heard about Jesus coming into town and she apparently knew a little bit about Him. As He passed by, there was a huge crowd gathered around Him. Remember, she had to be careful what she did as anything or anyone she touched was considered unclean. She had a choice right there. She could let her opportunity walk right by or she could take a chance. She could call out to Him, risking not being heard and risking being shamed and put down by the onlookers. She could try to position herself in front of Him, hoping He would run into her. On the other hand, and what she ultimately did do, she could sneak up behind Him.

A moment ago, I called this woman "lionhearted." Why would I say she was lionhearted if she didn't even have enough nerve to speak with Jesus? She actually snuck up behind Him, apparently on her hands and knees, and grasped the bottom of his robe. This woman was taking a chance that the most of us could never fully understand.

Touching the Hem

It was one thing for her to inadvertently touch someone, but to purposely place her hands on someone was intentional, and would be viewed as provocative too. Don't forget, Jesus had followers, and as such was seen as a teacher or a rabbi. This means He would have been viewed with the greatest of respect, and to touch Him with a known condition like this was borderline blasphemy.

To take this just a step further, she didn't touch Jesus just anywhere. She could have touched His arm, His leg, or some other part of His robe, but she touched the hem of His garment. In the Old Testament there was very specific protocol as to how a priest was anointed for service.

Oil was poured over the head of the priest. The oil was very thick and ran over their hair, down their beard and onto their robe. As gravity pulled the oil downward towards the ground, the oil continued to flow down the garment. It passed over their chest, move down their midsection, and down towards their legs. As the oil continued to run, it finally ran out of fabric at the bottom of the robe or hem. The hem got saturated with it as the anointing oil had nowhere else to go.

When this woman touched the hem of Jesus' garment, it wasn't because she was unable to reach any higher on His person. She was reaching for the anointing! She was expressing her openness to receive supernatural healing and formally recognizing Jesus as the anointed priest of God.

Do not forget that she herself was unclean. This woman was not permitted to touch a priest with her known condition, but she had reached a point of desperation. A desperation that had hit rock bottom, and knew no other way to receive what she needed. Now the "what if's?" come into play. What if I'm not healed when I touch Him? What if the crowd sees me on the way to Him and humiliates me? What if He sees me and refuses to allow me to touch Him? She could have easily missed her opportunity.

This precious woman would not be stopped. She refused to allow culture, religion, people, past failures, hurts, disappointments, sickness, or even the Mosaic Law to keep her away from her healing. This was her "go big or go home" moment! She had nothing to lose and everything to gain. This is real faith. She refused to be denied, and this is mountain-moving, lionhearted faith.

Notice what Jesus says in response to her actions. Jesus asked the crowd, "Who touched Me?" Jesus, Creator of the world and everything in it, obviously knew who touched Him. He did not say this for the purpose of gathering information. He was creating a teachable moment for those standing by. As the people began to quickly look around, searching for the violator, I'm sure this woman's heart was beating out of her chest. Had she been caught? Would she lose her healing? Would she be shamed, or worse, subject to religious judgment? What was the Rabbi about to say?

She did not hide. She told Him the truth.

Jesus said, "Daughter your faith has made you well." Did you catch that? Not your bold move to touch Me has healed you. Not your determination to press through an unruly crowd has healed you. Instead He said, "Your faith has made you well." The faith He references was the lionhearted faith of a woman who was tired of being told no; faith that was willing to press in, press through, and press beyond anything that would try to keep her from her blessing.

This woman wasn't a warrior; she wasn't even the picture of religious perfection. In fact, from what we know, she had most likely been distant from the things of God for many years. Her strength wasn't in what you could see in her outward appearance. Her strength was deep within her. Her strength wasn't in her name, a name known around the world, a name with family legacy or wealthy ties. In fact, the Bible never even mentions her name.

The lack of a name in no way discredits her. The reason her name isn't mentioned is so that only her faith is the focus of her story. Your name may not mean much to people, but I can promise you, it means the world to God. A woman with a twelve-year sickness with no money and no friends had the heart of a lion; she moved the hand of God.

Your name may not mean much to people, but I can promise you, it means the world to God.

You may be thinking, *I don't have that kind of heart.* You may be right, but guess what? You can develop it. It may be that this woman could have been healed years earlier, but maybe it took her twelve years to develop the kind of faith required for such an incredible miracle. The twelve years she was hurting, the twelve years she was rejected, the twelve years she was a social outcast, were twelve years she was growing in her faith.

While she was buried in discouragement, God was working inside her. While Ehud was deep in frustration over the treatment of His people, God was building something inside him. Every day he spent sharpening his sword was another day that God was pouring faith and strength into him. Each day that he rehearsed the "big-moment" in his mind was another day that God was expressing His love toward him.

The lionhearted aren't perfect; they are simply bold enough to believe God when it is the hardest to do. Right now, you may be experiencing major discouragement. Don't confuse the emotion of discouragement with the reality of small faith. In the middle of your discouragement is where you are poised to find your faith. When you're on top of the world, faith is an added bonus; when you're hurting and in need, it becomes a necessity. For Ehud, being lionhearted wasn't a luxury, it was a necessity. If he didn't have enough faith to kill Eglon, who would?

> The lionhearted aren't perfect; they are simply bold enough to believe God when it is the hardest to do.

The left-handed warriors of our day will not be people who tiptoe around issues, fearing a backlash. These warriors will stand for truth regardless of the cost. They will fight, even if they have to do it alone. They won't be weak-kneed or spineless; they won't run at the sound of danger. They will be people full of faith and full of heart. They will have their minds renewed; they will know where their faith lies. They may not be physically strong, or even superintellectual, but they will have an unwavering trust in their God. They will be regular people: They will be young and old, some will be orphans, others will be adopted, and they will be of every race and culture. They will all be uniquely different from each other. Though they will be very diverse, there is one characteristic they will all have in common: They will be lionhearted.

Chapter 7: The Chubby King

Chapter 7: The Chubby King

The story of the left-handed warrior contains some gut-wrenching details. As you read Scripture and realize the importance of what is being said, it is vital to know that the story doesn't contain unnecessary information. Sometimes, we read and think to ourselves, *Why would God take the time to share these specific words?* Know this: the totality of Scripture has been given for divine purpose. We don't often understand it, especially upon first glance, but it is all there for a reason. Such is the case, in this story.

> "So he brought the tribute to Eglon king of Moab. (Now Eglon was a very fat man.)" (Judges 3:17).

Why does the size of Moab's king have any relevance to this story? Is the writer obsessed with personal appearance? Does he write this simply for our own amusement? I believe Eglon's size was relevant to the story as it not only gives us a better mental image of what happened, but also sheds some light on a deeper meaning.

Eli: The Chubby High Priest

The Bible does mention this subject more than once, and as I read the story of Eglon, I can't help but remember another person in Scripture who was known to be very heavy. Eli was a high priest and judge of Israel during the time that Samuel was called to be the prophet of the nation. Israel was under siege by the Philistines, and after a heavy military exchange, Israel was overcome by them.

This battle was significant, not just due to the loss of life, but because the ark of the covenant was captured in it. The very presence of God was now gone, and the peoples' sense of protection, as well as future victory were very much in question. This created a strong uncertainty about the future, and caused great fear over what was to come. The loss of the ark wasn't the result of one mindless soldier, charged to protect and defend it. The loss of the ark was actually a long time coming, due to the indiscretion of God's people and their unwillingness to obey God completely.

This, just like the story of Ehud and Eglon, took place before Israel had a king. The nation was governed by judges, and the high priest was the key figure over religious practices. Eli was both high priest and judge, but was far from being a strong leader. In fact, he had allowed gross compromise within the priesthood itself. The real problem in the nation could not only be blamed on the people, but on Eli himself. Eli's own sons, Hophni and Phinehas, who were priests, acted in a way that brought dishonor to the priesthood and to the Lord.

> "Now the sons of Eli were corrupt; they did not know the Lord. And the priests' custom with the people was that when any man offered a sacrifice, the priest's servant would come with a three-pronged fleshhook in his hand while the meat was boiling. Then he would thrust it into the pan, or kettle, or caldron, or pot; and the priest would take for himself all that the fleshhook brought up. So they did in Shiloh to all the Israelites who came there. Also, before they burned the fat, the priest's servant would come and say to the man who sacrificed, 'Give meat for roasting to the priest, for he will not take boiled meat from you, but raw.'
>
> "And if the man said to him, 'They should really burn the fat first; then you may take as much as your heart desires,' he would then answer him, 'No, but you must give it now; and if not, I will take it by force.'

> "Therefore the sin of the young men was very great before the Lord, for men abhorred the offering of the Lord" (1 Samuel 2:12-17).

Eli's sons were out of control. These men were actually stealing the meat intended to be sacrificed to the Lord. People brought their offerings and were forced into giving the priest the selection of his choice. The Israelites were fearful of these men, as they were threatened with bodily harm if they didn't comply. As bad as this was, their sin didn't stop here.

> "Now Eli was very old; and he heard everything his sons did to all Israel, and how they lay with the women who assembled at the door of the tabernacle of meeting" (1 Samuel 2:22).

The magnitude of their sin is almost unbelievable. Not only were these men strong-arming worshipers into surrendering meat, but they were actually committing fornication. This fornication wasn't taking place in a hidden location like the back bedroom of someone's home either. It was happening at the very door of the tabernacle! Eli was aware of it, but he didn't do anything to stop it.

That's shocking. As the high priest, it was his duty to remove them from the priesthood. As judge, it was his duty to execute them. Eli only gave them a verbal slap on the wrist, and turned his head the other way. The sin continued until God Himself stepped in to correct it.

This brings us to the battle when the ark was captured. As a result of the sin in Eli's house, the entire nation had to suffer. The leadership was unwilling to take a stand and people were deceived, believing that God also turned His head and ignored wrongdoing. The Philistines were strengthened during this time period, and God used them to bring correction to His wayward nation. As the news of Israel's defeat was broadcast among the people, a sense of panic spread. When the message reached Eli, it was more than he could bear.

> "Then the man said to Eli, 'I am he who came from the battle. And I fled today from the battle line.
>
> "And he said, 'What happened, my son?'
>
> "So the messenger answered and said, 'Israel has fled before the Philistines, and there has been a great slaughter among the people. Also your two sons, Hophni and Phinehas, are dead; and the ark of God has been captured.'
>
> "Then it happened, when he made mention of the ark of God, that Eli fell off the seat backward by the side of the gate; and his neck was broken and he died, for the man was old and heavy. And he had judged Israel forty years" (1 Samuel 4:16-18).

As Eli heard about the defeat of his people, as well as the capture of the ark, he was crushed with an overwhelming sense of guilt. God had used young Samuel, who was only a child at the time, to give Eli a sinister warning. Eli knew what he was allowing to happen was wrong, but he didn't have the strength, courage, or energy to do anything about it.

A Spiritual Condition

Verse 18 points out that Eli was old and heavy. I believe that the mention of Eli's weight and age are relevant facts, and actually a key to the problems of the nation. Eli's physical attributes were an expression of the internal spiritual problem that he and the nation possessed. Eli's weight and age were an outward display of his stuck, immobile spirit that was slow to act as it ought.

As the priest and judge, Eli had the responsibility to act. As a matter of fairness, he had every opportunity to make the adjustments necessary, complete with a verbal warning from God's prophet. Eli's inability to be fluid and make the necessary hard choices gave God no alternative.

This leader was not functioning in any leadership capacity whatsoever; his refusal to make a choice became his choice.

It is easy to be stuck in a routine, and become comfortable in the rhythm of our lives. God, many times, brings circumstances and opportunities into our lives that will force us to make some adjustments. It's usually easier to keep doing things as we've always done them, but God has a way of forcing us into uncharted waters. As hard as the decision would have been for Eli, he knew the right thing to do, but was unable to bring himself to follow through with it.

There have been countless times in our ministry that God began to push us into completely new territory. These opportunities have never been without some obstacles, but obedience brings great reward. I want to challenge you with this: Don't let the inconvenience of obedience keep you from the possibility of your greatest reward.

Don't let the inconvenience of obedience keep you from the possibility of your greatest reward.

The fact that Eglon, king of Moab, was heavy is an important detail in this story. His, like Eli's, physical condition was an outward sign of his internal spiritual condition. Eglon's inability to break free from his generational idol worship was an immobility factor that set him up for personal disaster. Eglon didn't consider it risky to enslave and demand annual tribute from God's chosen people.

It is very easy for the mundane facets of our lives to become a spiritual noose around our necks. We can quickly become accustomed to our brief moments of religious experience, and instead of our walk with God being a daily adventure, we simply become vaccinated. A vaccine inoculates us from a disease by giving us small doses of the disease to allow our bodies to build up immunity.

Many believers today enjoy no challenge, no excitement, and very little—if any—risk. Church attendance, prayer, personal purity, and desire for growth all become secondary to the all-important tasks of the daily grind. Modern-day churchgoers have largely lost their burning sense of conviction and have been rocked to sleep by worldly pleasure and popular appeal. Many have become the spiritual equivalent of the chubby king: too satisfied to care and too immobile to adjust.

Modern-day churchgoers have largely lost their burning sense of conviction and have been rocked to sleep by worldly pleasure and popular appeal.

Killing the "Chubby King" in Our Lives

The only way for the Hebrew people to enter into their place of blessing and national prominence was to assassinate this heavy king. He couldn't be negotiated with nor could he be swayed by the cries of the people. There was no other way to close this painful chapter of Israel's history than to put a permanent end to this sadistic and ungodly king.

The king is the one who calls the shots, so to speak. In those days, a king's order was final. There was no appellate court system or other arm of government to filter his laws through. Much like the kings of those days, we are the decision-makers of our own lives. We control what we believe, we control what we give our lives for, and we make the final decision about how we invest our lives.

We cannot afford to be the chubby version of a believer who has been vaccinated against a true passion for God. Israel needed success. The only way for this to happen was for someone to kill the chubby king. We cannot negotiate with our passion either, nor can we negotiate with the Devil. The moment you sit down at the negotiating table with the Enemy, you've already lost. I want to challenge you to take an inventory of your spiritual life. Take the temperature of your spiritual fire. Be honest. Have you grown cold and weary of serving Jesus?

We cannot afford to be the chubby version of a believer who has been vaccinated against a true passion for God.

The spiritual immobility and slowness to action has to be killed. It took a man like Ehud to see this reality. Some in the nation may have believed that in time things would just get better. Some probably held on to the stories their parents told them of how things used to be back in the good ol' days: days of peace when they had a sense of national pride, when they were full of hope. Those nostalgic stories seemed a million miles away now as their new reality was living under an evil and overbearing Moabite strongman.

Ehud was different though. Sure, God raised him up, but Ehud still had a choice to be obedient to the Lord or rebel and shy away from his calling. It would have been much easier for Ehud to pass the buck and wait for God to raise someone else up. But the left-handed warrior had a sense of duty and responsibility that would not allow him to walk away from his eternal destiny. For the people to ever again enjoy the hope they once had, the king had to die—and Ehud knew he was the man to do it.

Are you ready to kill the chubby king? The chubby king of our life isn't an evil foreign dictator, but the person calling the shots in what we do with our lives. The chubby king of our lives is the person we see looking back at us in the mirror. That's right. Our immobility and slowness to respond can't be blamed on anyone other than ourselves.

There are always contributing factors to our current reality. Divorce, bankruptcy, sickness, misunderstandings, and even death may have some influence in the way we deal with, and respond to, life's playbook. Like Ehud in his heroic moment, we have to take a stand and be able to move beyond our hang-ups and take action. No excuses, no blame shifting, no procrastination, just action.

Taking Action

Years earlier in Israel's history, there was another time where procrastination kept the people from entering into God's blessing. The people had been led to the wilderness and God was working in them, not only to give them the Law and religious protocol, but also to prepare them for the battle that lay ahead. Moses knew the people would struggle with progress, and he knew that progress came at a price. He set up his inspirational speech with a reminder of what God had promised His people.

> "The Lord our God spoke to us in Horeb, saying: 'You have dwelt long enough at this mountain. Turn and take your journey, and go to the mountains of the Amorites, to all the neighboring places in the plain, in the mountains and in the lowland, in the South and on the seacoast, to the land of the Canaanites and to Lebanon, as far as the great river, the River Euphrates. See, I have set the land before you; go in and possess the land which the Lord swore to your fathers—to Abraham, Isaac, and Jacob—to give to them and their descendants after them'" (Deuteronomy 1:6-8).

He told them, "Turn and take your journey"; this is precisely what Ehud did when he faced the evil king. He realized the nation had been in bondage for far too long; he knew there was freedom beyond the struggle; he knew he could succeed with the help of God. In Deuteronomy, Moses encouraged the people that now was the time to take action. The "chubby king" of wilderness wandering and uncertainty had lasted long enough. Now was the time to kill inaction and possess the Promised Land.

The Promised Land had been promised for generations, and it was time for the people to dwell in the land He had prepared. Don't allow yourself to be rocked to sleep by inactivity; now is the time to enter into the promises of God. Now is the time to move into God's purpose and walk in the fulfillment of all that He has prepared.

Just like Ehud, we have an assignment. Each person's assignment is individually given and will not look the same. Some people have been called to politics, some to business, some to full-time ministry, and many other things, but what we have in common is this: We are all called to be obedient to the Lord. Other people didn't have the assignment of Ehud, Moses, Eli, or others. God never straps us with an assignment for the purpose of failure. He always plans for our success.

How to Kill the "Chubby King" in Your Life

I want to outline a few steps that will help with killing the chubby king of spiritual complacency. These steps are easy to understand but can be a little more difficult to live out in daily application.

1. **Deepen your place of worship.**
   Remember that Ehud's name indicated that he was a man of praise. David also found the true secret to growing deeper in the ways of the Lord by learning how to praise Him from the depths of his heart. This is the kind of praise that is only found in a face-to-face encounter with the Father.

This is the kind of praise that is only found in a face-to-face encounter with the Father.

> "Bless the Lord, O my soul; and all that is within me, bless His holy name!" (Psalm 103:1).

The psalmist says, "and all that is within me." This is a depth in praise that goes beyond the shallow waters. This is the type of praise that moves you close to the heart of God and comes from deep within you. Memorized words to a song can be of some benefit, but when your worship goes past the memorized and into the overflow of the heart, intimacy with God is truly ignited.

2. **Pray like your life depends on it.**

   I tell people this because your spiritual life *does* depend on your prayer life. We see Jesus modeling prayer often, and if Jesus felt like prayer was important, so should we. In the garden of Gethsemane, Jesus strongly reminds His disciples of the need for prayer when they began to be overcome with drowsiness.

   > "Watch and pray, lest you enter into temptation. The spirit indeed is willing, but the flesh is weak" (Matthew 26:41).

   Jesus tells His disciples a very important key to spiritual growth. He says, *"The spirit is willing, but the flesh is weak."* The key to overcoming our flesh is prayer. The disciples were physically tired, sleepy, and needed rest. Jesus' prescription was simple: Pray! Prayer keeps us from temptation, as overcoming the flesh requires a strong focus on godly action. Our spiritual tiredness can be overcome through prayer too.

The chubby king of complacency feeds on a lack of prayer.

Prayer is sometimes relegated to the leftover parts of our day. We hustle to work, study, go to school and other important activities every day, and if we're not careful, prayer gets lost in the shuffle. Spiritual strength requires prayer as a priority. Prayer cannot be a rarity. The chubby king of complacency feeds on a lack of prayer. When we don't get a heavenly download on a daily basis, we are missing the most important key to our own spiritual growth.

This is one of the areas I encourage people to set some personal goals. Maybe you set a goal of spending a certain amount of time in prayer, or while at a specific place. As you begin to speak to God and hear Him speak to you, it will create a hunger inside of you for more. The more you pray, the more you will desire that time with Him. You'll realize that nothing can replace the time you have with the Father each day.

3. Immerse yourself in God's Word.

The Word of God is the only Word that will always bring forth powerful results. Man's word is subject to failure, because man isn't perfect. God is.

> "So shall My word be that goes forth from My mouth; it shall not return to Me void, but it shall accomplish what I please, and it shall prosper in the thing for which I sent it" (Isaiah 55:11).

Daily study of, and meditation on, God's Word will become the actual foundation for your spiritual house to those who will deepen themselves in it. God's Word is eternal and life-altering. The heavens and the earth were created when God simply spoke. The planets aligned, the atmosphere was created, and man was designed, all at the response to God's Word. His Word not only encourages us, but His Word actually makes our faith stronger.

His Word not only encourages us, but His Word actually makes our faith stronger.

> "So then faith comes by hearing, and hearing by the word of God" (Romans 10:17).

Our faith is always under assault. The weapon of the Word strengthens and encourages us to never give up. Set aside time each day, to not only read the Word, but to pray over and think about what you've studied. God's Word will come to life within you, usually at times you don't even expect. You will find yourself talking to someone who needs guidance, and suddenly, the Word will begin to flow out of you. You will recall verses and stories you forgot you even knew.

The Word is alive, and gives us the strength we need to slay the overweight king of complacency.

When you combine these three elements: praise, prayer, and God's Word, you have the total package of strength you were intended to exercise.

When you combine these three elements: praise, prayer, and God's Word, you have the total package of strength you were intended to exercise. Ehud killed the chubby king, overcoming years of national complacency. He heard what God said, and he was crazy enough to believe and act on it. Don't be robbed of your intimacy with God. Rise up and kill the chubby king of complacency.

Chapter 8: Misdirection

Chapter 8: Misdirection

One of the oldest offensive football plays in a coach's playbook is the misdirection. This play works by the offense sending the signal that the ball is moving to one side of the field, while it is actually going to the opposite side. The linemen, the backs, and even the quarterback take at least a step or two to one side and then quickly readjust to run the ball the other way. The defense, who has been trained to watch and respond to offensive cues, can easily take the bait and move the wrong way. This error can cost the defense crucial seconds in play development and allow the offense many successful yards.

The misdirection play is designed to intentionally send the wrong signal and get the defense to respond inappropriately. This play has been used by football teams for decades, and if properly executed, can give the offense great success in moving the ball forward. This play is designed to confuse the reactionary instinct of the defense. The defensive team's strength, speed, conditioning, and desire to win become pointless if their initial response to the play is incorrect.

How many times have we fallen for the misdirection play in life? Sometimes we respond too quickly to something that happens, or we fail to respond when we actually should have. There are different reasons for that: Sometimes we're afraid to make the wrong decision, and other times we may not realize the severity of the situation. Whatever the reason, it leaves us regretting our incorrect decision or lack of action. Such was the case with Ehud's brilliant plan to assassinate the wicked King Eglon.

A Change in Plans

Eglon was surrounded by men who were responsible for his safety and well-being. These men were highly trained and screened to make sure their intentions and responses were up to par. As Ehud approached the king's inner chamber to deliver the tribute money, he would have been heavily profiled. The men were watching his every move and listening to every word that came out of his mouth. As covered in chapter five, Ehud was patted down to make sure he wasn't concealing a weapon, but as you now know, he was successful in smuggling his homemade dagger.

Ehud followed the protocol of paying the annual tribute. Most likely, this tribute would have been brought with a lot of fanfare. In ancient cultures, when tribute was brought, the people in the city were invited to watch. It was designed to celebrate the dominance of the receiving nation and to humiliate and further intimidate the paying nation. There may have been music, performers, additional military presence and a ton of nosey onlookers. For Ehud's plan to be successful, he had to give the impression that everything was normal. Everything would take place the same way it had during previous years.

Only Ehud knew that this time would be far different from any prior year. This time, there would be a change of plans that would echo throughout history. This time, Ehud would walk in bold obedience and dare to believe that Israel's future would never be the same again. As Ehud followed the proper procedures, he stood before the king, exchanged the customary formalities, paid the tribute, and now entering from stage left, the misdirection.

> "And when he had finished presenting the tribute, he sent away the people who had carried the tribute. But he himself turned back from the stone images that were at Gilgal, and said, 'I have a secret message for you, O king'" (Judges 3:18-19).

As Ehud delivered the customary tribute, as an inferior nation, he asked his entourage to leave as he turned back to the king. There is, however, a quick little blurb in between sending the people away, and speaking to the king. It says simply, "He himself turned back from the stone images that were at Gilgal." This sentence isn't just given for perspective; it carries significance as to Ehud's mindset while carrying out his plan. Before we can fully understand the implications of this sentence, we need to see the origin of these stones at Gilgal.

The Stone Images

Years earlier, Joshua was given the overwhelming responsibility of leading the entire race of the Hebrew people. He, of course, was taking over the leadership position that was left vacant after the death of Moses. Joshua's first major obstacle was to get the people across the Jordan River. This was important as this was the dividing line between the wilderness they had wandered in for forty years and the land of Canaan that had been promised to the people for generations.

As Joshua approached this important boundary line, he encouraged the people to be strong and have faith in the Lord. He told them that God would do wonders in their sight and show Himself strong on their behalf. As Joshua led the people, the priests were placed in the front of the processional. These men who carried the ark of the covenant stepped into the waters of the Jordan, and the river immediately stopped flowing. This was a miracle of truly biblical proportions, reminiscent of the Red Sea crossing led by Moses.

It's very unfortunate, how quickly we can forget the blessings of God.

The Lord understood how important it was that this miracle was remembered for generations to come. It's very unfortunate, how quickly we can forget the blessings of God. To commemorate this miraculous crossing, God gave Joshua very specific instructions to pass on to the men of Israel.

> "And it came to pass, when all the people had completely crossed over the Jordan, that the Lord spoke to Joshua, saying: 'Take for yourselves twelve men from the people, one man from every tribe, and command them, saying, "Take for yourselves twelve stones from here, out of the midst of the Jordan, from the place where the priests' feet stood firm. You shall carry them over with you and leave them in the lodging place where you lodge tonight."'
>
> "Then Joshua called the twelve men whom he had appointed from the children of Israel, one man from every tribe; and Joshua said to them: 'Cross over before the ark of the Lord your God into the midst of the Jordan, and each one of you take up a stone on his shoulder, according to the number of the tribes of the children of Israel, that this may be a sign among you when your children ask in time to come, saying, "What do these stones mean to you?" Then you shall answer them that the waters of the Jordan were cut off before the ark of the covenant of the Lord; when it crossed over the Jordan, the waters of the Jordan were cut off. And these stones shall be for a memorial to the children of Israel forever'" (Joshua 4:1-7).

From each tribe, a representative was selected to carry a stone from the riverbed to the other side of the Jordan. These stones were intended to memorialize the miraculous crossing and to answer the question: "What do these stones mean?" These stones were to be a constant reminder of God's power revealed to the Hebrew people.

It is believed that these stones had been carved by the heathen nations to represent their own false gods. If this is correct, this means when the Israelites saw these stones, the once powerful reminder of God's grace had now become defaced and sought to reduce the power of the God of the Hebrews. So when the children asked what the stones meant, the answer could become quickly convoluted and unclear. The stones of Gilgal were always a reminder of God's hand on the Hebrew people, but that meaning was now being threatened. Perhaps only the older generation could remember the true meaning of that once powerful memorial.

Realizing God's Ability

As Ehud turned from the presence of King Eglon, he faced the stone images of Gilgal and turned back to address the king. Ehud said, "I have a message for you, O king." This message, depending on the outcome, would be either life-threatening or life-changing for the Hebrew people. Ehud glanced at the stones, and we can only speculate as to what went through his mind at the time. Looking at these stones may have given Ehud a shot of adrenaline as he realized what God had the ability to do. Maybe he viewed himself as a man on a mission for the children, knowing that someone had to act or the foundation of the nation's faith could be lost forever.

If we're not careful, we can get so deeply distressed from our troubles that we fail to remember that God has always come through for us in the past.

Whatever went through his mind, Scripture records this for a reason. It is important for us to always remember what God has done for us. If we're not careful, we can get so deeply distressed from our troubles that we fail to remember that God has always come through for us in the past. In the seasons of national pain and discouragement, these stones were meant to remind the people that there was a God who cared for them. He was a God of limitless power who could even control the waters of the earth. No task was too difficult, no obstacle too big for God when He intervened on behalf of His people.

As Ehud's eyes met the stone images, he too was reminded of God's great strength, and the power he would now have to rely upon. The Devil most likely tried to dissuade him one last time. When he saw those images, Satan probably assaulted Ehud's mind with images of defeat. Satan would have tried anything to get Ehud's focus to quickly veer away from the hope of success and be blinded by the possibility of defeat. For Ehud, though, these stone images, like the final flag on the last lap for a race car driver or the two-minute warning for a football game, served as a reminder that he had come this far and victory was in plain view.

No Turning Back

Ehud turned from the stone images and addressed the king directly, saying, "I have a secret message for you, O king." The king, in his arrogance and pride, simply could not resist the possibility of finding out some sort of juicy nugget that could propel him to even greater notoriety. In violation of all security protocol and procedure, he sent everyone out of the room, everyone, that is, but Ehud. Now Ehud had his moment. He was alone with the oppressive Moabite king. Here the misdirection ploy becomes manifest, as Ehud reached for the concealed dagger strapped to his right thigh. The king leaned forward in avid anticipation of this secret message. Ehud, true to form, delivered that message and thrust his dagger deep into the belly of the wicked king.

Now Ehud had to act quickly. There would be no turning back, no second chances, no rethinking his plan. Ehud had to follow through and try to escape undetected.

> "Then Ehud went out through the porch and shut the doors of the upper room behind him and locked them.
>
> "When he had gone out, Eglon's servants came to look, and to their surprise, the doors of the upper room were locked. So they said, 'He is probably attending to his needs in the cool chamber.' So they waited till they were embarrassed, and still he had not opened the

> doors of the upper room. Therefore they took the key and opened them. And there was their master, fallen dead on the floor" (Judges 3:23-25).

Ehud locked the doors and escaped through a back entrance. The king's attendants waited for a long period of time, assuming he was taking care of personal needs; by the time they unlocked the doors and entered the room, the king had been dead for a long time. This provided Ehud with the much-needed window of time necessary to escape back to his people and rally the troops for battle.

Sometimes we associate Satan with the misdirection play. He loves to entice people with empty promises in order to get them to make fatal mistakes. Although that is certainly true, there is no greater master of the misdirection play than God Himself. When God uses it, though, it is never for the purpose of manipulation or confusion. He uses it to bring us closer in alignment to Him. God doesn't misdirect us; He misdirects Satan. Here's how it works: Satan brings disruption into your life: pain, anxiety, difficulty, and the like. God, who never takes the bait and becomes fearful, steps in and takes what was designed to hurt you and turns it into your greatest blessing!

As a football team sometimes falls for the misdirection strategy and runs their defense the wrong way, Satan wants us to get blinded by our circumstances and do the same thing. Satan wants us to run to discouragement, doubt, fear, or worse: He wants us to give up and quit. The people of Israel were at this place of completely giving up and quitting. For eighteen years they had been oppressed and in bondage. This was their reality; this was Satan's misdirection. What they did not realize was that God was raising up a left-handed warrior who would run a misdirection play of his own.

Scripture teaches us what I like to call the turnaround principle. This principle is very simple: Whatever Satan wants to use to destroy you, God desires to turn around for you. The Word tells us that mourning is only temporary.

> "Weeping may endure for a night, but joy comes in the morning" (Psalm 30:5).

Why is that? Is that because God is somehow insensitive to our needs and He's somehow telling us to hang in there and suck it up? No, this means that God is saying, "Your weeping is a temporary state; it's a season. I will bring joy back into your life."

If you're in a place of deep pain or sorrow, know this: God is very aware of your situation and committed to restoring your joy. Satan is trying to keep you focused on movement going the wrong way. God is vying for your attention and faith so He can bring about His plan in your life.

God is saying, "Your weeping is a temporary state; it's a season.

Keep Focus Like David

In the classic story of David and Goliath, we see much focus on the size of Goliath and his impressive track record of past victories. Young David steps out on the battlefield to fight this giant, and it was obvious he was outmatched. He would need a miracle to win or he would go down in history as another notch on the Philistine giant's belt. As David approached Goliath, he kept his focus on the Lord and refused to be manipulated by any misdirection. His brothers told David that he should go back home and take care of the sheep. King Saul told him that he was too young and inexperienced to tangle with a warrior like Goliath. Just the size of Goliath alone was intimidating and overwhelming for all who were about to witness this epic battle.

> "And a champion went out from the camp of the Philistines, named Goliath, from Gath, whose height was six cubits and a span. He had a bronze helmet on his head, and he was armed with a coat of

> mail, and the weight of the coat was five thousand shekels of bronze. And he had bronze armor on his legs and a bronze javelin between his shoulders. Now the staff of his spear was like a weaver's beam, and his iron spearhead weighed six hundred shekels; and a shield-bearer went before him. Then he stood and cried out to the armies of Israel, and said to them, 'Why have you come out to line up for battle? Am I not a Philistine, and you the servants of Saul? Choose a man for yourselves, and let him come down to me. If he is able to fight with me and kill me, then we will be your servants. But if I prevail against him and kill him, then you shall be our servants and serve us.' And the Philistine said, 'I defy the armies of Israel this day; give me a man, that we may fight together.' When Saul and all Israel heard these words of the Philistine, they were dismayed and greatly afraid" (1 Samuel 17:4-11).

David wasn't intimidated by Goliath's size or his impressive record. David kept his focus on the Lord. This was the source of David's strength, and this is why David won. You know how this story ends: God took a little shepherd boy and empowered his arm and a sling to kill the mighty giant. God can take anybody and empower him or her to do anything. As impressive as this is, there's an even greater truth found in this story.

God can take anybody and empower him or her to do anything.

Before David killed Goliath, he was an unknown shepherd boy from the small insignificant town of Bethlehem. He had few friends from what we are told, no connections in high places, and, without a doubt, he was no celebrity. Remember though, David had been anointed some time earlier by Samuel the prophet to one day be the king of Israel.

Samuel was instructed to go to Jesse the Bethlehemite's home, and there he would find the man that God selected. This would not be a man judged by the criteria created by other men, but rather the person that God Himself had both chosen and prepared.

> "But the Lord said to Samuel, 'Do not look at his appearance or at his physical stature, because I have refused him. For the Lord does not see as man sees; for man looks at the outward appearance, but the Lord looks at the heart.'
>
> So Jesse called Abinadab, and made him pass before Samuel. And he said, 'Neither has the Lord chosen this one.' Then Jesse made Shammah pass by. And he said, 'Neither has the Lord chosen this one.' Thus Jesse made seven of his sons pass before Samuel. And Samuel said to Jesse, 'The Lord has not chosen these.' And Samuel said to Jesse, 'Are all the young men here?' Then he said, 'There remains yet the youngest, and there he is, keeping the sheep.'
>
> And Samuel said to Jesse, 'Send and bring him. For we will not sit down till he comes here.' So he sent and brought him in. Now he was ruddy, with bright eyes, and good-looking. And the Lord said, 'Arise, anoint him; for this is the one!' Then Samuel took the horn of oil and anointed him in the midst of his brothers; and the Spirit of the Lord came upon David from that day forward. So Samuel arose and went to Ramah" (1 Samuel 16:7-13).

How in the world could an unknown, small-town shepherd boy ever be accepted as the leader of an entire nation? If nobody knew him, how would anyone ever follow him? How was David going to get from the shepherd's staff to the king's scepter? In the natural this would be impossible, but God took what Satan planned to destroy David and used it to fulfill His purposes.

> What Satan designs to destroy you, God can use to promote you.

If David had choked when he faced Goliath, perhaps running off the battlefield in fear, the people only would have known him as the man who was afraid to fight. But because David was successful, he now had the attention of not only the king of Israel, but the entire nation. Always remember this: What Satan designs to destroy you, God can use to promote you. Satan planned for Goliath to be the end of David, but God planned this conflict for his beginning.

Most people love a good underdog story. The people were so impressed with David's later victories that they even wrote a song about him.

> "So the women sang as they danced, and said: 'Saul has slain his thousands, and David his ten thousands'" (1 Samuel 18:7).

Can I tell you that there are incomplete songs about your life? Even as you read these words, there are songs being written by heavenly choirs about your exploits. Satan tried to intimidate David from ever hearing his song, but God turned it around! Don't let the Enemy steal your song; your season of mourning will come to an end.

Were it not for the giant named Goliath, David would have never have been king. God took his adversity and turned it into victory. This is God's specialty. Satan will play on your problems, but never fear: God is taking your problems and exposing them for the misdirection they are. God isn't confused or even mildly worried; God is turning it around.

Disaster or Stepping-Stone?

When I was studying for the ministry, I lost my job. I had been working in construction and the company was downsizing. They were forced to terminate several jobs. As a fairly new employee, that meant that

I was one of the ones who was let go. I'll never forget that day as I walked into the office to the time clock and found that my time card wasn't there. I was informed that I was no longer needed, effective immediately. My first reaction was one of disappointment and even anger. At least I could have been given a little time to find another job! Instead I was terminated with no warning and no severance pay.

I remember going out in the parking lot and trying to get my thoughts together. I didn't want to drive home and tell my wife the bad news so I just began to pray. I asked God to help me and lead me to a place where I could begin working as soon as possible. All of a sudden, a business I had passed on my way to work popped into my mind. I hadn't really entertained any thought of applying at this place before. Before today, as far as I knew my job was secure and things seemed to be going pretty well. After some back and forth reasoning, I decided to drive over and see if I could talk to someone about a job.

I walked into the business and shared my situation. The young woman at the front counter was very nice and asked me to take a seat while she called the manager. The manager came in and conducted an on-the-spot interview with me. I expected him to say, "We'll keep you mind, and if anything comes up, we'll let you know," but he offered me a job on the spot. In fact, he asked if I could begin working immediately, to which I replied, "I can start right now!"

Sometimes it's in perceived defeat that you find your greatest victory.

This already seems like a pretty good testimony, but there's more: The new job paid me more money and gave me more benefits than the job I previously had. Looking back, I realize this was no coincidence. The Lord was beginning to teach me a life-changing principle: Sometimes it's in perceived defeat that you find your greatest victory. Were it not for me being fired, I would have never seen the opportunity for a better job.

Ehud's entire future and the future of the nation hinged on Ehud's misdirection. Ehud employed one of the oldest tricks known to man. Eglon expected one thing, but Ehud delivered another. Things are not always as they seem. God specializes in the turnaround. What looks like disaster may be your next stepping-stone. The Devil may believe he's got you right where he wants you, but the Lord is working on the misdirection play. Don't let people confuse you by their assessments based on what they see in the natural. God sees the big picture, the whole picture. He is an offensive mastermind and He specializes in taking your defeat and turning it around.

Chapter 9: Pull the Trigger

Chapter 9: Pull the Trigger

I often use the phrase, "Pull the trigger!" It means to go ahead and do it already. "It" being whatever it is that you are thinking of doing. People often spend a lot of time, sometimes, an entire lifetime, contemplating an action that never happens. I wonder how many best-selling books, award-winning songs, marriage proposals, and the like will never be seen because the trigger was never pulled. The proverbial "trigger" represents that moment of no return when you plunge ahead into a decision, when there is no turning back.

This is the "I do" of a wedding ceremony, the signing on the dotted line of a contractual agreement, or the plunge into the frigid waters for your first swim of the season. When you pull the trigger on a gun, you cannot put the bullet back into the barrel. Once the trigger is pulled, the bullet has been spent and there is no way to undo what has been done.

I have had many of those moments in my life, but there is one in particular that I will never forget as long as I live. It was my birthday, and my precious daughter wanted to do something for me that I would always remember. She wanted to take me skydiving. Well, mission accomplished! She had me drive to a small hidden airport about an hour and a half from our house. I didn't know where we were going, as it was a surprise until the very last minute.

She was navigating with the GPS on her phone and giving me turn–by-turn instructions. All the while I was completely oblivious to her grand scheme. As we approached the little airport, my daughter asked, "Do you have any idea what we're going to do?" My answer was no, but about that time, we turned a corner and I saw a sign that said, "Skydiving: Two miles ahead." I quickly looked at her with wide eyes, and she began to laugh. I knew right then that we were headed for trouble.

She asked me, "Do you want to do this?" I was scared stiff, but I sure wasn't going to chicken out in front of my daughter. So with the best, deep, confident Daddy voice I could muster I said, "Sure!" Even though I think my voice crackled a little, I really tried to sell my confidence.

As we walked into the place, the very first thing they told us to do was sign a thick stack of liability release forms. As I read over the agreement, there was the subtle mention of such minor things as paralysis, broken bones, and death. I looked over at my daughter. Without hesitation, she was signing away. I can't tell you I wasn't having second thoughts, but I had to be the big, brave Daddy, so I signed as well.

Next we were taken into a room where we watched a training and safety video. As I watched this video, I couldn't help but think about things like: *Is my life insurance up to date? Would my wife be okay in my absence?* I knew that statistically skydiving had a relatively low rate of incident, but I was sure those "incidents" never ended well for the diver. After all, an airplane is designed to transport people between locations. When I watched movies, the only time I saw people jump out of planes was when they were headed for a crash. Now here I was, paying money to jump out of a perfectly good airplane!

After the video we were each strapped to an instructor and settled into the plane. Within a short couple of minutes, we were airborne and on our way. It seemed to happen so quickly. I was never able to really look my daughter in the eye and make sure she really wanted to go through with this. As the plane was noisily ascending into the air, I looked at her and mouthed the words, "Do you still want to do this?" She gave the thumbs up, so I knew, like it or not, it was going to happen.

When we reached the proper altitude, the instructor scooted us to the edge of the plane. I remember my heart was beating so loudly I could hear it throbbing inside my head. The instructor yelled to me, "Are you ready?" I knew that when I said yes, it was all over; there would be no turning back. I looked over at my daughter once more, and she gave me her big beautiful smile. I said, "Yes, let's go!" With that word, I was immediately careening face down towards the earth at an incredible rate of speed.

The jump was actually a lot of fun after the initial feeling of *what have I just done?* It was very beautiful seeing the ground from a bird's eye view. After we both landed, I spoke with the instructor who was tethered to me. I commented to him that when I said "Let's go," he jumped immediately. I had been sort of expecting a countdown or an *Are you sure?* or something, but no, when I said yes, we jumped. He told me that was the time people chickened out. He said that when he gave people additional time after the initial "Are you ready?" question, many times people panicked and chose not to jump. Their policy was that when they got the green light, don't give the client a chance to back out.

The Point of No Return

That experience was one of my pull-the-trigger moments. Once I jumped out of the airplane, there was no turning back. I couldn't push a rewind button and return to life before the jump. Just like the bullet that can't be put back into the gun, once the skydiver jumps out of the plane, they must now adjust to their decision. In the story of Ehud, there was a turning point in the events of that memorable day.

As Ehud approached King Eglon, he also had a pull-the-trigger moment. Before the actual assassination, he could have quit at any time. As far as we know, Ehud hadn't told anyone of his intentions, so there was no worry of disappointing or creating confusion among the people who were with him. As he handed over the tribute money, Ehud's heart was racing, his palms were sweaty, and his stomach was in knots. He knew that this one moment could never be redone.

The faith and surety inside of Ehud's heart helped him move forward and not back down because of the future unknown. He had only one chance to get this right and once he passed the point of no return, he would be either a hero or a dead man. For Ehud, there would be no turning back. He had formulated a plan, he had prayed it through, and he had great confidence that God would make it successful.

I've seen many people's dreams die on the shelf. Most people have great intentions, and those intentions sound noble, even inspirational; but for those intentions to become realities, there has to be a shift from talking, thinking, and dreaming, to actual doing.

Most people have great intentions...but for those intentions to become realities, there has to be a shift from talking, thinking, and dreaming, to actual doing.

When I was a child, my grandfather owned a woodworking business. He custom-made clocks, tables, and the like. I worked with him for several weeks each summer to earn some extra money and learn the value of hard work. My grandfather often gave me a task that was much harder than I had ever done before. Sometimes it was relocating a large pile of wood or cleaning up after a tractor trailer had unloaded. I looked at those jobs and went into deep contemplation over the best way to accomplish them.

Oftentimes I circled around the pile of wood or other seemingly impossible task, trying to come up with a game plan. I wasted precious amounts of time trying to analyze the most effective course of action. I can remember my grandfather saying to me: "Jamie, stop 'politicking' and get to work!" What was he saying? You can analyze things for so long that you become counterproductive in your achievement. Many things do have to be thought through and carefully planned, but there comes a time when you have to pull the trigger and take action. That pile of wood wasn't moving itself, no matter how long I talked about it. At some point, somebody had to get his or her hands dirty and start taking action.

> You can analyze things for so long that you become counterproductive in your achievement.

Time to Step Out of the Boat

Peter's life was definitely illustrative of this principle. If anything, Peter may have been a little too quick to take action, without properly thinking things through. There needs to be some balance in how we approach planning and action, but Peter certainly serves as a good example of "pulling the trigger."

> "Immediately Jesus made His disciples get into the boat and go before Him to the other side, while He sent the multitudes away. And when He had sent the multitudes away, He went up on the mountain by Himself to pray. Now when evening came, He was alone there. But the boat was now in the middle of the sea, tossed by the waves, for the wind was contrary.
>
> "Now in the fourth watch of the night Jesus went to them, walking on the sea. And when the disciples saw Him walking on the sea, they were troubled, saying, 'It is a ghost!' And they cried out for fear.
>
> "But immediately Jesus spoke to them, saying, 'Be of good cheer! It is I; do not be afraid.'
>
> And Peter answered Him and said, 'Lord, if it is You, command me to come to You on the water.'
>
> "So He said, 'Come.' And when Peter had come down out of the boat, he walked on the water to go to Jesus. But when he saw that the wind was boisterous, he was afraid; and beginning to sink he cried out, saying, 'Lord, save me!'

> "And immediately Jesus stretched out His hand and caught him, and said to him, 'O you of little faith, why did you doubt?' And when they got into the boat, the wind ceased" (Matthew 14:22-32).

Jesus had sent the disciples away on a boat so He could have some time of solitude for prayer. The disciples obediently were in transit across the waters when the waves began to pick up as the result of high winds. As the disciples began to analyze their dilemma, off in the distance they saw a figure walking on the water and coming towards them.

At first, they were terrified, as it is somewhat uncommon to see such an incredible sight! Nevertheless, Jesus responded to their fear by confirming that it was Him. Now I hesitate in this moment briefly. I think most people in this same situation might respond a little differently than Peter did. It would be natural for someone to say something like, "Jesus, how are You doing that?" or "Why are you doing that?" Yet Peter, also known as "the trigger puller," responds completely differently. Instead of a "normal" response, Peter yells out, "Lord, if it is You, command me to come to You on the water." What kind of response is this? This is the response of someone who is accustomed to taking action.

There were many times when this behavior got Peter into trouble. He often put his foot in his mouth and angered the other disciples, and even drew some rebukes from Jesus. He wasn't the most sensitive guy, but he was a man of action and he was not afraid to pull the trigger. In the garden of Gethsemane, Jesus was surrounded by Roman guards, about to be arrested. According to the gospel of John, one of the disciples actually pulled out his sword and cut off the ear of the high priest's servant. If you're thinking Peter was the culprit, you would be right.

Peter had this proclivity to take action. He was willing to act in faith, sometimes prematurely, but he could never be accused of being a passive person. This behavior was many times reckless, and perhaps this swinging pendulum of reserved versus unrestrained boldness was a little heavy on the boldness side. However, Peter's quick reaction and fast response moved him into a place of experience with Jesus that few other disciples ever had.

On that windy evening, the disciples watched Peter engage Jesus and invite himself out on the water. Can you believe the daring and sheer nerve Peter must have possessed to make such a wild statement? "Lord, if it is You, command me to come to You on the water." I bet when he made that statement, the other disciples looked at each other and thought, *Here we go again. Big mouth Peter is jumping in without thinking again.* Then, the story gets even better: Jesus responds to Peter and simply says, "Come." Jesus had to be laughing on the inside; He knew full well where this was headed. It's one thing to say something and then quickly regret what you just said, but this statement had the potential of being a little more dangerous than pulling your foot out of your mouth.

I wonder what was going through Peter's mind after he made this brash request. I have to believe that when those words, "If it is you, command me to come to You on the water" came out of his mouth, he was instantly humiliated and filled with regret. I bet he wanted to somehow quickly erase the fact that those words were ever said. For a guy like Peter, his bigger issue was that the other disciples heard him say them. Now no matter what happened, Peter, like a kid being challenged with a dare on the playground, had to make good on his proposal.

Peter made this outlandish statement, probably thinking, "Jesus will never let this happen" but Jesus did. Jesus beckoned Peter, this wild-eyed, big-mouthed, reckless fisherman, to step out of the boat. Why would anyone step out of a perfectly good boat into the dangerous waves of the sea? This action makes no sense; it is dangerous, even potentially life-threatening, and at the very least, embarrassing.

Taking all of this into account, or maybe not taking any of this into account at all, Peter actually does it. He steps out of the safety of the boat in order to take a risk in the unknown dangerous waters of the Sea of Galilee. What if I fail? What if I'm humiliated in front of the other disciples? What if I'm remembered for the rest of my life by the results of this action? None of this swayed Peter's decision; he was pulling the trigger, and that was that.

What happened next has been widely discussed, and even ridiculed, as people seem to focus on Peter's perceived failure. Yes, when Peter stepped out of the boat and into the water there was a lack of faith as he realized the dangers of the deep. Peter was distracted by the size of the waves and lost sight of the size of his God. I have heard countless sermons exhorting us to not do as Peter did, and always keep our eyes on Jesus. This is definitely a great takeaway from this story and worthy of attention, but there is a bigger message that is often overlooked.

Peter's Water Walk

I have always wanted to ask the folks who like to ridicule Peter for his lack of faith one simple question: "Have you ever before walked on water?" That is a fair question because Peter is the only person in the Bible, other than Jesus, who actually did. True, his water-walking experience was short, possibly as short as a few seconds, *but he did walk on water*. Even though it was a brief experience, it was a real experience; and it was Peter's experience. It was an experience that would have never happened had he been unwilling to pull the trigger.

Once Peter stepped out of the boat, there would be no return. The sea is unforgiving and holds no hostages. Had Jesus not saved Peter, he would have drowned that starlit night. As a result of Peter's faith, though fleeting, we can read the story of a man who did what no other man ever did in all of history. I can't criticize Peter for his failure; I'm in too much awe of his trigger-pulling faith.

What if the other disciples had petitioned Jesus to do the same? What if all twelve of these guys had gotten out of the boat and began to exercise their faith? What if all of them would have been encouraged by Peter's powerful demonstration of faith and chosen to take the same step he did? We will never know the answer to that question, because they, unlike Peter, didn't pull the trigger.

As Peter was rescued by Jesus, and had to take the walk, or swim, of shame back to the boat, I wonder what the other disciples were thinking. Were they embarrassed as a result of his flamboyant behavior? Were they impressed with his short-lived stint of water-walking? Or more appropriately, were they embarrassed by their own lack of faith, slowness to respond, and unwillingness to challenge their boundaries and get out of the same boat he had exited?

Like the gun, once the bullet has been discharged, Peter's step out onto the water could not be undone. This is the very thing that keeps us from stepping out into the unknown. We tend to "What if?" ourselves to the point of inaction. If Peter's fear of drowning was bigger than his faith in Jesus, he would have stayed put. It makes a lot of sense to stay put, because "staying put" means safety and the lack of challenging the sure thing. The Christian faith, however, isn't built on staying put, it is built on radical, trigger-pulling faith.

The Christian faith, however, isn't built on staying put, it is built on radical, trigger-pulling faith.

Note that Jesus' rebuke of Peter was very mild, almost endearing: "O you of little faith, why did you doubt?" We are not told that the other disciples chimed in too by rebuking Peter. They were probably ashamed of their own lack of faith to get out of the boat themselves. Peter's willingness to be a "trigger puller" opened doors for his life that were opened for few others.

Peter was one of the only three to witness the transfiguration of Jesus (Matthew 17:1-11). Peter was the one who was challenged by Jesus to allow his testimony to become the very foundation for the church in its early development (Matthew 16:18). Peter was also the only disciple recorded whose shadow healed people (Acts 5:15), and the first of the Twelve directed to preach to the Gentiles (Acts 10).

Keep Dreaming in Spite of Failure

How is it possible that the sinking disciple had such an incredible journey of faith? Just like on the windy waters of the Galilean Sea, Jesus reached down and picked Peter up every time he fell. Peter didn't let his past failures keep him from taking future chances. Peter made some big mistakes, even colossal ones some might say, but Peter kept moving forward, despite the pain of the past.

Don't let your dreams stay dormant because of unpleasant past experiences. One of the things I tell the guys in our organization is: "If we're not making any mistakes, it means we're not being aggressive enough." If you've never failed, it means you've never tried anything too difficult. Peter was rebuked, and then the strong, loving hand of Jesus reached down into those frigid waters and picked up the discouraged disciple. That wasn't the end though: Peter kept believing; he kept stepping out, he kept taking chances.

If you judge your willingness to pull the trigger by the criteria of past failure, you may never have the audacity to dream again. Jesus was a risk taker. Who did He choose as His original twelve disciples? One was a tax collector, several were fishermen, one was a doctor, and don't forget, one of them was a thief and a betrayer. The fear of failure didn't keep Jesus from investing in these men. Judas, who would ultimately betray Jesus, was given responsibilities like the other disciples. Jesus even ministered to him during the Last Supper, like the others. He even went so far as to wash his feet, just like the others.

If you judge your willingness to pull the trigger by the criteria of past failure, you may never have the audacity to dream again.

Was this risky? You better believe it, but it didn't keep Jesus from pulling the trigger. Maybe you've wrestled with something over the years, and for whatever reason, you've talked yourself out of taking the risk. Maybe a new business, a relationship, going back to school, or applying for that hard-to-get job. Whatever it is, don't let your past mistakes or pain keep you from the possibility of future joy.

You have the pleasure of using every product you enjoy because someone took a risk in developing and marketing it. Every church you've ever attended was there because someone stepped out in faith, believed God, and started a brand-new church. Every marriage you see attests to the fact that two people were willing to take a chance on lifelong commitment to each other. Most anything of any value required a substantial amount of risk at some or many points. The fear of failure is the lack of ability to know that God will pick you up when you fall. Just as Jesus picked up Peter in that embarrassing moment of failure, He will always pick you up too.

Some people, to a fault, are too quick to act, while others won't act until it becomes absolutely necessary. This is when true faith comes into play. If I am acting recklessly and bringing pain and disruption into my life, I have a faith problem, meaning this: I'm acting on my own behalf, and not truly hearing the voice of God. On the other hand, when I'm stuck in a rut and not moving anywhere, that is also a faith issue. If I have the faith to hear God and obtain His dream for my future, then I need to exercise that same faith to step out and let Him bring it to pass.

In the story of Ehud, there were many times along the way that I'm sure the Devil was filling his mind with doubts. He could have easily quit at any time: in his preparations, in his prayer time, and even when it was time to actually follow through with the assassination. Like Peter, who really wanted to get out of the boat, Ehud really wanted to make a difference in his nation. Peter had the boldness to trust in Jesus, though briefly, to do what others would never dare. Ehud had that same joy, the joy that comes from a victory when the odds are stacked against you, the joy that can only be obtained through great accomplishments.

When Ehud laid his head down on his pillow that night, though he was sore and stiff from battle, I know he felt incredible. No regrets for Ehud; no "what if's?" and no "I wish I would have..." or "If only I had the guts to…" What he did have instead was a great sense of accomplishment and a completed faith-filled venture only made possible by the grace and strength of God.

God puts dreams in us for a reason, not to just allow them to marinate without purpose.

That feeling of satisfaction will never come as long as the dream sits on the shelf. As long as you're content with just talking about it or imagining what could potentially happen, you'll never be fulfilled. God puts dreams in us for a reason, not to just allow them to marinate without purpose. He plants dreams, ideas, and possibilities in us to see if we will allow our faith to embrace His plan.

I don't know how the original idea came to Ehud. He may have had a dream, a vision, or simply a God-inspired idea. Somewhere along the line, though, that idea began to take shape. It moved beyond a good-sounding proposition to a well-planned, multi-faceted, and strategic mission. Ehud moved slowly enough to develop a solid plan, but quickly enough to act in a timely manner, before the dream had a chance to expire. Exactly how all of this came together, we'll probably never know; but one thing we know for sure, none of this would have ever happened if Ehud had not pulled the trigger.

Chapter 10: Who Are You *Again*?

Chapter 10: Who Are You *Again*?

I have to confess I'm a highly impatient person. I can't stand long lines, traffic, or having to wait on hold for someone to answer the phone. I'm able to hold it together for a brief period; but if my wait is too long I become anxious and a little irritated. I've prayed about this over and over, and I believe God is helping me, just not as quickly as I'd like! As a result of this, I always dread having to call businesses to handle changes or adjustments to any account I may have with them.

Most people have had to deal with a credit card company at some point. After you spend what seems like an eternity in phone-prompt no-man's land, if you're lucky, you are eventually able to speak with a live person. When this person answers, you are then led through another long list of questions in an effort to confirm your identity. You may have to tell them the last four digits of your social security number, your address, your phone number, your mother's maiden name, or your little brother's nickname when he was five. Finally, after they are convinced that you are the person you claim to be, the person on the other end of the line says, "Now, how may we help you?" This process is more than a little aggravating, but it is a necessary evil that can potentially prevent someone from making changes to our account, or worse yet, stealing our identity.

Identity is Linked to Faith

Knowing who you are is the foundation of operating in the power of faith. If we are not sure of who we are, we will never have confidence in the power that we represent. In His ministry to the disciples, Jesus was very emphatic that they had a clear understanding of who they were. In the days following Jesus' resurrection from the dead, He challenged His disciples to act in the power of their identity. There are clear signs that will accompany and follow the believers in Christ.

> "Later He appeared to the eleven as they sat at the table; and He rebuked their unbelief and hardness of heart, because they did not believe those who had seen Him after He had risen. And He said to them, 'Go into all the world and preach the gospel to every creature. He who believes and is baptized will be saved; but he who does not believe will be condemned. And these signs will follow those who believe: In My name they will cast out demons; they will speak with new tongues; they will take up serpents; and if they drink anything deadly, it will by no means hurt them; they will lay hands on the sick, and they will recover'" (Mark 16:14-18).

First, there is a rebuke against their unbelief and hardness of heart. Next, Jesus informs them of their responsibility to proclaim the gospel to all who will hear. Then, Jesus lays out a few interesting points to outline the areas of both responsibility and authority that the believer possesses.

If we are not sure of who we are, we will never have confidence in the power that we represent.

He says, "they will cast out demons" and "they will speak with new tongues." This area of authority is over the spiritual realm. Casting out demons is not something that is done by the power of natural man. We can't prescribe medication that will rid someone of demonic influence; they must be prayed for and cleansed by the power of the Spirit. God has given us great authority in the spiritual realm. This authority does not come through our own power, but the power of the Holy Spirit that operates within us.

Next, Jesus says, "they will take up serpents; and if they drink anything deadly, it will by no means hurt them." This outlines the authority the believer has against attack in the natural world. This is speaking to those areas in which Satan tries to intervene in our lives by coming against our finances, our homes, and anything else we face in our day-to-day routine. This is very broad but it is demonstrative of how God determines that the Enemy should not push His children around in the natural.

Finally, Jesus says, "they will lay hands on the sick, and they will recover." This details the authority we have to operate in the gifts of the Spirit. The natural man cannot heal; only by the power of God's Spirit and His special touch are we able to experience God's healing power. Therefore, Jesus is saying that we have the privilege to allow healing to flow from Him, through us, and to others.

Delegating Authority

It is important to understand that authority can be released to others by simple delegation. I have a vehicle, which has my name on the title. This vehicle is registered in my state under my name, and as such, I have the responsibility to drive it safely, and the authority to do so. However, the keys are in my possession. You can't drive a car without the keys, so the keys now become the proof of permission. If I release my authority by allowing one of my kids to carry the keys that means they have been given, by delegation, my authority to operate that vehicle. Even though I am the rightful owner of the vehicle, as such I can allow others to function under my authority and drive my car.

The authority we possess as believers isn't ours because we are all powerful. The Father has released His authority to us. We've been given permission by Him to operate under His name and carry out His purposes. It's His power and authority, but it has been given to us as believers; and it carries great responsibility. In Matthew, Jesus spoke to Peter about the future of the disciples and the church. Peter, as a fledgling disciple, was eager to understand his boundaries, but he knew there was a great deal of work to be done. Jesus commissioned Peter to future ministry with the following statement:

> "And I will give you the keys of the kingdom of heaven, and whatever you bind on earth will be bound in heaven, and whatever you loose on earth will be loosed in heaven" (Matthew 16:19).

Much has been said by many preachers and theologians regarding the keys of the kingdom. But there's one thing of which we can be sure: The keys represent authority. The holder of the keys has access into doors, locked gates, vehicles, and anything else that has restricted access. Jesus was saying to Peter, "I am releasing kingdom authority for you to use to further My purpose." Jesus was explaining to Peter that as long as he operated under the authority of Christ, Jesus would back him up.

That is a powerful concept. Jesus is literally telling Peter, "I've got your back!" That sheds a whole new light on our faith and how God views our willingness to fully trust Him. In effect, Jesus is saying, "If you'll be faithful to step out in faith, I'll always be there to make sure that My strength will go with you." Peter knew that regardless of how unstable the political or religious scene became; Jesus would be his faithful friend and his source of strength.

He will never let us down. He has never gone back on His Word; He has never overpromised and under-delivered.

Friend, I want you to know that Jesus always has your back. He doesn't agree to stand on your behalf if you're in sin or way outside of His direction; but when we're in obedience to Him, He will always fight for us. God is always faithful. He will never let us down. He has never gone back on His Word; He has never overpromised and under-delivered.

Our God is mighty; and He loves us and promises to protect us and guard us from evil.

Just like Jesus didn't throw the disciples out in the cold and expect them to fend for themselves, He doesn't expect us to stand against the Enemy all by ourselves. He doesn't partially equip us either; He equips us with authority over spiritual powers, over attacks in the natural, and then gives us the strength of His spiritual gifts to be successful.

Holding on to the Promises

Before David became king of Israel, he was running from the crazed and jealous, mad King Saul. God was faithful to David over and over again. Many close calls in the natural were averted simply because God stepped in. By all accounts, David should have been dead! Saul had the strength of the entire army of Israel behind him, and David was only one man. Yet God showed Himself faithful to the up-and-coming anointed king of Israel. As David reflected on God's favor over his life, he wrote the following words in Psalm 18:

> "The Lord is my rock and my fortress and my deliverer; my God, my strength, in whom I will trust; my shield and the horn of my salvation, my stronghold" (Psalm 18:2).

David knew the faithfulness of God, not just because someone had told him about it. He knew about God's faithfulness because he had seen it demonstrated continually in his own life. How could David have this kind of faith? How could a young shepherd boy be willing to stand toe-to-toe with a giant? How could he maintain his confidence and trust in the Lord when King Saul had a price on his head? How could he continue to write songs of praise to God, knowing that at any moment someone could interrupt his praise with a flying arrow? David's confidence came from knowing who he was!

God had anointed David to be the future king; David held on to that promise. I want to encourage you to hold on to the promises that God has given you too. I hope you're beginning to realize who you are. You are precious in the sight of God and you were purchased with an extremely high price tag. Paul exhorted the Corinthian church not to think like natural men. Because of who they were, they were to be different.

> "You were bought at a price; do not become slaves of men" (1 Corinthians 7:23).

The truth of the matter is this: We have an advantage over the people of the world. Those who are unbelievers, though loved by God, are not in alignment with God. As a result, there is a disconnect between His grace and what they see and understand day-to-day. However, we are redeemed by Him, purchased with His own blood. We have the advantage of walking in the grace and power of our Father.

When we question or doubt who we are, it is a challenge to our very identity. My kids are now at an age where they are out and beginning their own lives. Even though they are married and are beginning their own families, we are still connected by blood and by our relationship with each other. My kids don't have to ask permission to come into my home. They don't have to ask to grab something from the refrigerator. They don't have to ask to use our bathroom. Why not? Because they are our children, and as such they have permanent access into our home.

Great Authority=Great Responsibility

As God's children, we have been entrusted with great authority, which in turn also carries a great responsibility. We cannot forfeit our authority and allow ourselves and others to be overrun by the Enemy. God has given us real authority that enables us to be successful and see His kingdom power released on the earth.

> "God has work to do in this world; and to desert it because of its difficulties and entanglements, is to cast off His authority. It is not enough that we be just, that we be righteous, and walk with God in holiness; but we must also serve our generation, as David did before he

> fell asleep. God has a work to do; and not to help Him is to oppose Him." ~ John Owen[16]

Think about what it would be like if someone close to you left you an inheritance upon their passing. Maybe they leave you their house or property; they have given that to you because they love you. If you chose not to use that gift; if you let the property remain abandoned and become uninhabitable; what would that say about the way you value that gift? What would that say about your willingness to honor them and the relationship you had with them?

God released His authority to the believer because He loves us and wants us to prosper in His kingdom.

God released His authority to the believer because He loves us and wants us to prosper in His kingdom. To deny that power is to go against the very fabric of God's intention for us. Jesus gave His life for us to walk in an understanding of God's grace that could not be found by simple obedience to religious dogma; He brought us into a relationship of trust and love.

Don't Wait to Step Out

In the story of the left-handed warrior, Ehud chose to embrace the responsibilities that were placed on him. He could have very easily determined that someone else should be the one to take the lead on this ambitious plan. Surely there was someone who would be better suited for this gutsy move, but there was something deep in the heart of Ehud that would not allow him to shift the responsibility to someone else. I

16. Pamela Rose Williams, "Top 15 Christian Quotes About Authority," What Christians Want To Know RSS, 2015, accessed October 09, 2017, http://www.whatchristianswanttoknow.com/top-15-christian-quotes-about-authority/.

believe he knew that if he failed to step up to the plate, he would always live in regret.

I don't know Ehud's specific skill set. He was obviously very clever, intentional, and brave, but I don't know what else he was gifted in. It would be presumptuous to speculate on his areas of strength, but I do know that he carried a deep sense of calling and responsibility to right some wrongs done to his people. Maybe Ehud had always thought someone else would rise up and kill King Eglon; maybe he thought that the wicked king would have a divine intervention and have a change of heart. Perhaps, he waited until he couldn't wait anymore, and like Isaiah the prophet said, "Here am I! Send me" (Isaiah 6:8b).

We will probably never know exactly how all of this came about, but Ehud had a great deal of confidence in his ability to be successful. How do we know that? We know because he carried out the plan. If he lacked confidence in the plan, his own insecurity would never have allowed him to follow through. His confidence was not founded in his inherent abilities as a successful assassin. He had never assassinated anyone before. His confidence came from knowing that God was with him, and that God was for him.

This man isn't known to have a huge following of people who supported him, or that determined to go with him and fight alongside of him. By all accounts, his only real source of support was from the Lord Himself. As we have no record of an angelic visitation or no record of a vision or a dream, my sense is that Ehud found the plan of God as he sought after the Lord in his pain and sorrow over the treatment of the Hebrew people.

One of the things I've learned in dealing with people over the years, is that many have a tendency to wait for that "burning bush" moment. We want God to write a message in the sky or visit us with an angel, proclaiming the direction of God. Well, friends, my experience is that normally God's plan doesn't unfold that way. I have very few in-my-face God is speaking to me moments in my life. When God begins to speak to me, and gives me a game plan, or gives me hope in the midst of crisis, I usually find that while being quiet and attentive to Him.

WHO ARE YOU *AGAIN*?

The prophet Elijah was a man known to be bold, brash, brazen, and quick to "tell it like it is." He's the one who prophesied to King Ahab that it wouldn't rain on the earth except at his word. Elijah was the one who had the famous showdown on Mount Carmel when he called fire down from heaven, after which he led God's people to kill hundreds of false prophets and priests of Baal.

Elijah saw great success when these prophets and priests were eradicated from the earth, but he still had a problem. The wicked King Ahab and the possibly-more-wicked Queen Jezebel were not very impressed by Elijah's fiery miracle. Elijah left the mountain not as a victor, but deeply afraid of what would happen next. Elijah began to cry out to the Lord, and God was faithful to respond to His fearful prophet.

> "Then He said, 'Go out, and stand on the mountain before the Lord.' And behold, the Lord passed by, and a great and strong wind tore into the mountains and broke the rocks in pieces before the Lord, but the Lord was not in the wind; and after the wind an earthquake, but the Lord was not in the earthquake; and after the earthquake a fire, but the Lord was not in the fire; and after the fire a still small voice."
>
> "So it was, when Elijah heard it, that he wrapped his face in his mantle and went out and stood in the entrance of the cave. Suddenly a voice came to him, and said, 'What are you doing here, Elijah?'"
>
> "And he said, 'I have been very zealous for the Lord God of hosts; because the children of Israel have forsaken Your covenant, torn down Your altars, and killed Your prophets with the sword. I alone am left; and they seek to take my life.'"
>
> "Then the Lord said to him: 'Go, return on your way to the Wilderness of Damascus; and when you arrive, anoint Hazael as king over Syria. Also you shall anoint Jehu the

> son of Nimshi as king over Israel. And Elisha the son of Shaphat of Abel Meholah you shall anoint as prophet in your place. It shall be that whoever escapes the sword of Hazael, Jehu will kill; and whoever escapes the sword of Jehu, Elisha will kill. Yet I have reserved seven thousand in Israel, all whose knees have not bowed to Baal, and every mouth that has not kissed him'" (1 Kings 19:11-18).

When God began to speak, there was an incredibly strong wind, so strong in fact, that it literally tore into the rock face of the mountain upon which Elijah was standing. The story is very clear, "the Lord was not in the wind." Next, the ground began to shake under the stress of a great earthquake, but again we are told that God wasn't in the earthquake. Finally, there was fire that came from heaven; now we're speaking Elijah's language, but no, the Lord wasn't in the fire either.

Remember, Elijah was this strong, brazen prophet who was used to making a dramatic splash: God had performed miracle after miracle through his hands. These three natural calamities: wind, the earthquake, and fire, were simply designed to get his attention. This was the language that Elijah spoke: big, loud, attention-drawing, causing a scene, but God wasn't speaking through any of these means. Then we see something completely different than what we (or Elijah, for that matter) would expect.

A still small voice began to speak to the hurting prophet. After God got his attention with all the natural disasters, Elijah was in a place to truly hear what God was saying. Notice the message behind the still small voice. Elijah was now attentive and hungry for reassurance and hope, and God speaks these simple words: "What are you doing here, Elijah?" Elijah had to be thinking, *What am I doing here? I'm running for my life!* What was God really saying to him? "Elijah, who are you?" God was reminding him that He had protected him all these years, and He would surely not forget him now.

As God continued to speak to Elijah, He gave him specific instructions about what he was to do next. At the end of that, God brought Elijah back to the core message. Elijah's initial fear and dramatic proclamation was that he now stood alone as the sole prophet of God. God proceeded to correct him: "Yet I have reserved seven thousand in Israel, all whose knees have not bowed to Baal, and every mouth that has not kissed him." God's message to Elijah was crystal clear: "I have all of this under control. My power isn't diminished in the least." The undertone was that God had it in control. He knew who He was, and His reminder to Elijah was, "Know who you are."

Be Willing to Listen

Elijah didn't get this message by way of the wind, earthquake, or fire. It was in the quietness of solitude in a cave instead. Too often, we want the razzle-dazzle of a booming voice from the sky to encourage us, direct us, or help us maintain our course. True communication with the Lord usually happens when we are all alone, when we empty our soul and we are willing to simply listen to His voice.

True communication with the Lord usually happens when we are all alone, when we empty our soul and we are willing to simply listen to His voice.

Again, we don't know the exact circumstances surrounding Ehud's direction from God to pursue this dangerous undertaking. I believe that in his desperation, he was exasperated about the condition of his people and he began to cry out to the Lord. The same almighty God who was faithful to bring the Hebrews out of Egyptian bondage was the same God that would refuse to abandon them now. God is the One who raised up the left-handed warrior. He breathed life and encouragement into him. Ehud's confidence was not in his great strength or in his ability to wield the sword; his confidence was in the Lord.

As Ehud walked into King Eglon's chambers on that fateful day, he walked in knowing his God, but also knowing his own identity. He wasn't just some wayward, idealistic soldier, trying to leave his mark in history. He was called of God, he was directed by God, he had met with God, and he knew full well who he was and what he was called to do. If Ehud didn't have self-confidence, he would have allowed his own fleshly fear to keep him from following through with his plan. Ehud could have panicked and given up his whole covert operation, had he carried one shred of doubt about who he was. Ehud knew His God, and Ehud was secure in his own identity.

The Enemy will always try to undermine our personal identity. He will try to get you to doubt not only your place in God, but also your own value. When you begin to doubt your worth, your faith is diverted into an endless road of worry and anxiety. When your confidence comes from the Lord, you have enough belief in His plan through you that you can take on things much bigger than you are. Make no mistake: God's power is our source, but we must also know who we are in order to fully embrace that strength.

When you begin to doubt your worth, your faith is diverted into an endless road of worry and anxiety.

In the Paul's message to the Corinthian church, he wrote:

> "Now thanks be to God who always leads us in triumph in Christ, and through us diffuses the fragrance of His knowledge in every place" (2 Corinthians 2:14).

Paul knew it was important for the believers to know that not only is Christ triumphant, but He is triumphant through us. God has chosen us to be His vessels; and because He chooses us, we are special to Him.

WHO ARE YOU *AGAIN*?

Regardless of how inadequate you may feel in your struggle, never forget who you are!

Satan is very skilled as an identity thief. He truly fears those who will recognize and accept who they are. As hard as you work on your own personal confidence, Satan works just as hard to undermine it. When God's people are truly confident in their God, they will also be confident in themselves.

> "What then shall we say to these things? If God is for us, who can be against us?" (Romans 8:31).

You cannot lose! You might be beaten up, bruised, and battered, but ultimately God is your strength. Regardless of who is against you, God is for you. Remind yourself daily of who you are. Tell yourself that you are special in the eyes of God. Don't ever forget your value; God certainly never will. Somewhere inside you lies a left-handed warrior, a person of promise, a person of destiny, and a person of victory. Who are you again? You are everything that God says you are, and that, my friend, is enough.

Chapter 11: Behind the Scenes

Chapter 11: Behind the Scenes

As a child, I watched different television shows and wondered, "How do they do that?" The shootouts looked so real in a good western or murder mystery. On the big screen, people being swallowed by avalanches or walking through fiery buildings looked so real. You know these people are actors and believe they are not actually harmed—or worse, dead—but it looks as if what you see on the screen is actually happening in real life.

We live fairly close to some world-famous theme parks. When you go into these parks during regular business hours, your eyes are forced to focus on the things they want you to see. They are very careful to keep unappealing sights well out of sight. Electrical wires, data cables, and trash cans are all brilliantly covered or somehow designed to blend in with the décor of the park. Those who work there tell us that during off-business hours, they are busy with street sweepers, pressure washers, and other maintenance items to keep the park looking its best. All of this is designed so that when the park opens the following day, everything is in good working order, clean, and in its proper place.

Therefore the excited, easily impressed, and (now broke) theme park visitor enjoys the park at its very best. The average observer thinks that everything just sort of fell in place. If the job is being done correctly, the visitors won't have any idea that ten to twelve hours of hard work just preceded their visit. As visitors enjoy all the rides, shows, cartoon characters, and more, everything behind the scenes, though necessary, is out of sight. The visitor's experience should not include having to worry about maintenance or custodial concerns; they are paying for family entertainment.

The park operators know that in order for families to be carefree and have the time of their lives, these aspects of park management need to be out of sight. As they say: A clean house can go unnoticed, but a dirty one is sure to draw attention. In the same way, a well-managed park experience should leave housekeeping items well below even the most astute person's perceptive radar.

God Is Working Behind the Scenes in Our Lives

God is the epitome of the behind-the-scenes coordinator. As in a Broadway performance, complete with sound, lights, and special effects, God is working behind-the scenes and taking care of areas of our lives that we have no clue about. He is working in places that we aren't even aware need His attention in the first place.

As in a Broadway performance, complete with sound, lights, and special effects, God is working behind-the scenes and taking care of areas of our lives that we have no clue about.

Such was the case with Ehud, the left-handed warrior. He was set aside before he even entered into the world. His parents did not know this boy would have God's destiny written all over his life. To them he was just another bouncing baby boy, their bundle of joy; but to God and to the Hebrew people, he would be much more.

> "But when the children of Israel cried out to the *Lord*, the *Lord* raised up a deliverer for them: Ehud the son of Gera, the Benjamite, a left-handed man. By him the children of Israel sent tribute to Eglon king of Moab" (Judges 3:15).

Israel had run out of hope, their affliction had now lasted for over eighteen years and they were tired. They were fearful of the Moabite people and had been preconditioned by their subservient existence. Before they ever prayed and repented of their sins, before they ever cried out to God for deliverance, God was working behind-the-scenes.

Ehud looked like just another young Hebrew boy, a boy who would grow up as a servant of Moab but who was actually in the beginning stages of God's unfolding plan. Ehud was no regular Hebrew boy; he was a boy that fit securely into God's plan to redeem His people, but only after they decided to change their ways. What they did not know was while they were living in sin, desperate and without hope, God was already formulating a plan for their escape.

You may find yourself in the middle of a story right now, not a story about someone else, but your story. The story you're in may currently be taking a path you don't really like. Like riding on a wild roller coaster, you may be nauseous as a result of the violent twists and turns your story has taken over your lifetime. You may be in a place right now where you say, "How in the world did I get here?" You may have never anticipated being in your present predicament. Remember that God is a specialist in working behind-the-scenes. Even if you've never cried out to Him before, whenever you do, He already has a plan in place; and not just any plan, but a plan to change the ending of your story.

He already has a plan in place; and not just any plan, but a plan to change the ending of your story.

Israel could never have dreamed up a plan like the one God designed for them. His plan was so simple, yet so brilliant that no military mastermind could have ever conceived it. They knew that their oppression had not allowed them to build up sufficient military strength to overthrow the Moabite people. They knew that their men would never be bold enough to rise up and overrun the city; there was too much fear in them that the years of oppression had spawned. Any plan they devised was quickly squashed by the reality of a hopeless people, who considered themselves doomed to a life of continued struggle.

God, however, is not limited by our way of thinking. He doesn't see things in the same way that we do. Man looks up from his limited resource and limited capability. Humanity can only see what lies directly in front of them, and has no vantage point of what lies ahead. On the other hand, God looks down with absolutely no limitations. With His resources and capabilities, His possibilities are limitless. His plans are perfect; His ways are without error; He is all-powerful and doesn't comprehend "can't" because He "can"!

Ehud's birth was just the beginning of God's brilliant plan as He worked behind-the-scenes to restore Israel's hope and freedom again. At some point, God began to share His plan with Ehud. His plan would require the would-be assassin to go in singlehandedly and kill the king of Moab. If Ehud was anything like us, he probably took some convincing before he ever bought into this daring assassination attempt.

We don't know exactly how all of this took place, but I have to believe that once Ehud began to think in terms of killing the king by himself, he probably doubted the likelihood of his success. As God's plans begin to unfold, they sound way too big for us. Our first feeling is often an overwhelming sense of fear. I have no doubt Ehud experienced some fear before, during, and after his great feat. Even so, God was working in the background to give Ehud the confidence he needed to follow through with God's plan.

God Is in Control

Scripture speaks to us about a peace that comes from God in the times when we need it the most. This peace goes beyond human reasoning; it makes little sense in the natural. It is a peace that reminds us that even if our calling leads us to smuggle a dagger into the king's chamber and risk our lives, God is with us from the beginning to the end.

> "Be anxious for nothing, but in everything by prayer and supplication, with thanksgiving, let your requests be made known to God; and the peace of God, which surpasses all understanding, will guard your hearts and minds through Christ Jesus" (Philippians 4:6-7).

The Lord knew that Ehud would be anxious about the wild endeavor; who wouldn't? He worked in an unseen manner to provide the peace and inner strength that would help him manage his own emotions and be immersed in the faith that only God could provide.

Remember that in your pain, hurt, and anxiety, God is aware of your emotional condition. He is working behind-the-scenes in you too: not just to bring about a successful resolve, but also to support and strengthen you during the unknown. God is not like the pragmatic thinker who is only concerned with getting things right; He views us with the love of a father. God doesn't just want us to succeed; He wants us to stay healthy during the process.

God doesn't just want us to succeed; He wants us to stay healthy during the process.

As brilliant as the left-handed warrior plan was, it still required additional favor from the Lord. In chapter five, we discussed how Ehud's left-handed dominance would have helped him tremendously as he was going through the king's security detail: His dagger was strapped to his right thigh and the security personnel probably had no experience with this before. Their focus was on his left side as he was checked before carrying the tribute to the king. Even though this was a great plan, it was certainly not fail-safe. Any bulge or gathering of his clothes could have led to an additional search. And then there's the fact that just because they hadn't seen a lefty before didn't guarantee they would not check his other side. Here's where God comes in again!

Our unseen and all-knowing God made sure that these complications didn't happen. Maybe there was a strange sound or other distraction just as the guards were about to check Ehud's opposite side. Perhaps one of them became impatient and signaled the security detail to hurry. We really don't know exactly what happened, but I can tell you this: When Ehud was given clearance to walk into the king's chambers he breathed a colossal sigh of relief!

Even our best plans will fall short if the grace of God doesn't step in. We can think things through, even rehearse our actions until we are sick and tired of rehearsing, but at the end of the day, our plans are just that, our plans. We can try, and when we fail, try even harder; but some things require a level of strength that we just don't possess. Here's where our God, who specializes in behind-the-scenes orchestration, enters our situation, cleans up our mess, smooths things over, and brings success.

Even our best plans will fall short if the grace of God doesn't step in.

I often travel to the nation of Honduras, as we oversee several churches there. The first time we went many years ago, we didn't know anyone there. Simple things like safe hotels, safe forms of travel, safe places to eat, and other arrangements all had to be carefully considered. I remember our first night there. I traveled with only my interpreter, and we ended up on a much-delayed flight. This put us in the area we were supposed to be staying in at close to 3:00 a.m. Although this area was relatively safe, it was definitely not ideal for Americans to be wandering around at that time of the night. Because we didn't know what else to do at the time, we ended up staying in a small hotel in the center of the town. We later found out that this particular hotel was known for a high crime rate, and was highly advised against.

The next morning (by chance, or so we thought) we ran into a local man at one of the coffee shops. He was a strong Christian and happened to be very well connected in the city. He had several family members, all key business owners in the city, and he took the time, with no expectation of anything in return, to take us around the city and introduce us to each of them. This put us into contact with a hotel owner, restaurant owner, pharmacy store, and more! Later we found out that this man owned his own bus. He became our driver as we took teams of thirty or more people into that area. That relationship with him still exists to this day, and we make sure to visit him every time we go.

There is no way we could have ever made this kind of strategic connection ourselves, especially on the very first morning of our trip. How did that happen? God was working in the background to make sure that we would be well cared for and safe. No brochure, no Internet search, no word-of-mouth information, no exertion of our own can produce what God produces when He is formulating His plans without our knowledge.

Counting on God's Help

We tend to get anxious and uptight about things over which we have little control. When we realize that He is continually working in areas that we don't see, we'll rest a little better and breathe a little easier. When our focus remains on the Lord, there is a great deal of confidence that He will work on our behalf. Jesus relayed this truth to His disciples in the Sermon on the Mount.

> "But seek first the kingdom of God and His righteousness, and all these things shall be added to you" (Matthew 6:33).

Jesus is saying, "Put Me first; do what only you can do, then I will always do what only I can do!"

Ehud saw God's unseen hand. He saw this in his own peace in the situation as well as his success in getting past the security detail, but now he needed some supernatural intervention more than ever. God's help had finally placed him in the room with the king. It was critical that everything would go right.

> "So he brought the tribute to Eglon king of Moab. (Now Eglon was a very fat man.) And when he had finished presenting the tribute, he sent away the people who had carried the tribute. But he himself turned back from the stone images that were at Gilgal, and said, 'I have a secret message for you, O king'" (Judges 3:17-19).

The money had to be delivered to the king with no hint of there being any additional agenda attached. Any sweaty palms, stuttering tongue, darting eyes, deep breathing, or other nervous behavior would have alerted the king that something wasn't right. Ehud's dagger and its placement could have easily shifted during the search or in walking into the king's chambers. All eyes were on the Hebrew deliveryman as he was presenting the tribute to the king of Moab.

Just thinking about this scenario makes me nervous! One slip of the tongue, a dagger that accidentally falls to the floor, or any obvious anxiety, and Ehud would have been a dead man. How could they have not known that there was a hidden agenda of some sort? How could a man walk right into the presence of the king with a deadly weapon, completely undetected? Ehud may have had nerves of steel, but God had blinded the guards and the king to any of the obvious signs before them.

When God is working behind-the-scenes in our favor, He takes a crazy idea with little chance of success and turns it into a reality.

God can do far more than we ever think possible. Most of us would never even dare to dream of a scenario like this. It's far too risky; the consequences of failure are far too great; the probability of final success is far too low. However, when God is working behind-the-scenes in our favor, He takes a crazy idea with little chance of success and turns it into a reality.

We usually imagine that it would require a great deal of strategy and a group effort for a subservient group of people to overtake an oppressive nation. We envision a drawing board, secret meetings in the middle of the night, undercover spies, and much more. We think in terms of a covert plan that involves planning, multiple points of entry, underground tunnels, a mole placed inside the evil kingdom, and an elaborate escape plan. They would never entertain a simple idea in which one man with one weapon killed the king by himself, and then escaped to gather the warriors of the nation. Nevertheless, this is how God worked then and now. He doesn't need an army; He doesn't need your theological understanding; He doesn't need your pristine track record. In this story He was only looking for an obedient left-handed man to carry out His plan. God knew He could take care of all the little details behind-the-scenes.

Do Away with the Waiting Game

Sometimes we fail to do anything significant for the kingdom because we are waiting for the grand master plan. We are waiting on this strategic planning masterpiece that will cover our every doubt and every concern. We are hoping that God's plan will be so perfect in our eyes that it will erase any of our reservations or any possibility of danger. Many times, we are waiting on someone else to do what God has called us to do.

Many times, we are waiting on someone else to do what God has called us to do.

Ehud couldn't afford to wait on someone else. God was looking for a left-handed warrior, and he knew that he fit the bill. For eighteen years, his people had been under duress, and the situation wasn't changing any time soon. Someone had to do what nobody else was willing to do. There are left-handed warriors who are reading these words right now. God is calling you to stop waiting on a perfect plan, a perfect person, a perfect scenario, and rise up and be what God has called you to be.

I want to be clear: I'm not taking anything from Ehud at all. I have to give him incredible respect for his bravery and obedience, but the truth is that God could have used anyone on the planet to do what Ehud did. God wasn't looking for the most gifted person, and He wasn't looking for a man with superior fighting skills, He was looking for a left-handed person who would believe God would work and do what he could not.

When I realize that God is working in the background of my life, it removes a lot of pressure.

When I realize that God is working in the background of my life, it removes a lot of pressure. As a pastor, I make multiple decisions every day, many of which carry significant impact on other people's lives. Those decisions weigh heavily on me and I try to be very careful and intentional about each of them. If I didn't know that God was working on my behalf in ways that I don't even realize, the weight would be more than I could bear. However, I know that God is working on my behalf; He's got my best interest in mind; He's concerned about me and what I do. I know that all that I do must be fully submitted to Him. I can't carry the pressure on my own. He has to help me, or I will fail miserably.

Years ago, we bought a large puzzle and put it on our dining room table. This puzzle was a very difficult nature scene, and we knew that this would be no easy task. Each night, or whenever we got an opportunity, we passed by it for a few minutes and would try to find a few pieces to add to the work in progress. My wife and each of my three kids, who were small at the time, all had a part in putting that puzzle together. There were times when we saw the kids looking at the puzzle in deep concentration as they searched and searched for a particular piece. We were under no time constraints to get the puzzle completed, but as it got closer to being done, the anticipation began to build. Each person wanted to be the one who had a part in completing the puzzle. What started as a curiosity soon developed into a full-blown obsession! One night, two of our kids were at the table working frantically on the puzzle.

I noticed that the puzzle was almost done, missing only a small portion. Before long the other child showed up, and then not to be outdone, my wife and I joined as well.

It was obvious that this puzzle would be finished within the next few minutes. Unbeknownst to us, my oldest son took one of the pieces and put it in his pocket. As we continued to work together, the anticipation of a finished puzzle was quickly building. We all added pieces, until finally there were only a few more pieces to go. You could tell by looking at the puzzle, that there was more spaces than pieces. Was it possible that the manufacturers sent out a puzzle that was short one puzzle piece? As the last couple of pieces were being set, my concern was confirmed: We were missing a piece! All the pieces we had were locked into place, and we were looking at a completed puzzle, all except for one lousy piece!

Everyone was looking under the box, under the table, under chairs, and anywhere else that the piece could have gone. After a minute or two, we looked at each other in frustration, as if we thought all of this work was for nothing. It was impossible to finish it without that missing piece. After all, what good is an incomplete puzzle? It was at about that time that my son got a big smile on his face. He reached into his pocket and pulled out the missing piece that was quickly, and happily, locked into its resting place. He then announced, "I just wanted to be the one to finish the puzzle." The rest of the family was not very impressed!

Like a puzzle, our life is being fit together by God. There are pieces that seem to be missing; there are others that don't seem to fit anywhere properly. Yet God is always working behind-the-scenes to put together the overall, beautiful and complete picture of our lives. Like my son, God has the final pieces in His possession. Our lives may look to us like a picture that will never be complete, but God will finish His masterpieces. He is just waiting for everything to line up.

God held the pieces to Ehud's puzzle. There were some things Ehud had to do in obedience to God, but there were other things that were outside of his ability to control. He could make the dagger, he could strap it to his right thigh, and he could try to gain access to the king. He could pull his sword and finish the job. All the other things, though, were outside his control; only God had the power to bring about his eventual success.

God Can Do What We Can't

The necessary, behind-the-scenes work doesn't stop there for Ehud though. Masterful and unseen choreography was in play as Ehud planned, got through security, and even asked for a private meeting. The tribute had been successfully delivered. Now Ehud's plan and God's backstage handiwork would collide for a story that will endure for centuries. All planning and favor reached an intense crescendo as Ehud extended his faith for this most important part of the plan.

> "But he himself turned back from the stone images that were at Gilgal, and said, 'I have a secret message for you, O king'" (Judges 3:19).

This is it! I can overhear the voice inside of Ehud's head, saying, "You really did it. There's no turning back now." There has to be more at play here than a king quickly agreeing to a private meeting with a potentially hostile foreign guest. I am not a secret service agent, but I would have to believe that this meeting between the king and Ehud broke all kinds of security rules. Anyone who would have witnessed Ehud's request probably expected the king to require additional security to be present in the room. Surely this was a bad idea for the king. Anyone would think so. Anyone, that is, except for someone who is familiar with the unseen God who is constantly at work to bring His plans to fruition!

What was the king thinking? Didn't he realize that this left him completely exposed to potential danger? What kind of message could this tribute-carrying Hebrew have that was so important that he would be willing to risk his own life to gain it? I'm really not sure what his thinking was, but it proved to be a fatal mistake. There had to be supernatural intervention for the king to completely disregard all decorum, let his guard down, and meet one-on-one with the man who was about to kill him.

God would not have brought Ehud this far to let him down now. He had been successful all the way up to this point; God would make sure that he would be successful in the end. Friend, know this: God is completely committed to you. God is in it for the long haul. His investment in you is too great to quit now. Paul reminds us of this as he writes an encouraging word to the church, while he himself is locked up in a prison cell.

> "Being confident of this very thing, that He who has begun a good work in you will complete it until the day of Jesus Christ" (Philippians 1:6).

While the room was being cleared to allow for the private meeting between Ehud and King Eglon, God was working. Perhaps He was stirring the prideful heart of Eglon, causing his mind to wander about the possibilities of this secret message. Maybe Eglon thought Ehud was going to defect; maybe he thought there would be more money involved. We don't know that answer, but there is no question that God set it into motion.

God is completely committed to you. God is in it for the long haul.

Now the room was free from inquisitive ears and eyes. Ehud moved close to the king, as to whisper in his ear. This was it. There was be no way to stop now. Ehud's heart raced. With a quick and steady motion he reached down and pulled the dagger, immediately thrusting it into the belly of the king. The king collapsed to the floor. Now Ehud had to escape. Ehud's plan was still in motion as he locked the doors behind him.

> "Then Ehud went out through the porch and shut the doors of the upper room behind him and locked them. When he had gone out, Eglon's servants came to look, and to their surprise, the doors of the upper room were locked. So they said, 'He is probably attending to his needs in the cool chamber.' So they waited till they

> were embarrassed, and still he had not opened the doors of the upper room. Therefore they took the key and opened them. And there was their master, fallen dead on the floor" (Judges 3:23-25).

The awkwardness of this private meeting played out as the guards waited by the doors. How did they not hear the king moaning and gasping as he was stabbed in the stomach? God was working behind-the-scenes. How did they not hear the doors lock? God was working behind-the-scenes. How was Ehud able to escape out of a window with nobody seeing him? Again, God was working behind-the-scenes.

The God who never sleeps is the God who is always working behind-the-scenes to cause us to succeed.

The God who never sleeps is the God who is always working behind-the-scenes to cause us to succeed. When you take into account the amount of supernatural intervention in this story, it is easy to realize that God is for us. From the very conception of Ehud as a child until the day the Hebrew bondage was broken, God was at work. Never forget that: God is working behind-the-scenes! You may not see it now, but eventually it will all make sense. Satan wants you to see the immediate impossibilities, but never give up! God is at work. Just because there's some obstacles doesn't mean God has abandoned ship. He is faithful, He is committed, and He has a strength and competency we can never fully understand.

Chapter 12: Cue up the Band

Chapter 12: Cue up the Band

Excitement and anticipation were in the air; the unspoken tension was so thick you could almost cut it with a knife. The stands began to fill with hopeful fans on either side to cheer on their favorite team. The smell of fresh cut grass, combined with the intense Florida heat and humidity, filled the air. The stadium lights were lit, the concessions were being cranked out at full capacity, the band was warming up, and the cheerleaders were stretching to perform their daring stunts. This was the night of the week we all lived for. It was Friday night football in a small town. This was more than just a sport; this was when the whole community came together to cheer on their beloved high school. It was game time!

As a high school senior, this would be my last season as a player, so each and every game had a high level of personal importance to me. This game, however, was even more significant as it was against one of our most fierce rivals. The team we were set to play had a slightly better record than we did, and we all knew that in order for us to win this game, everything would have to go our way.

The visiting team brought multiple buses packed with fans that night, so the grandstands were absolutely jammed with supporters on the visitor's side. The home team fan base came through as well. It would go down as a near-record crowd in our small town. This game would most likely be a nail biter, and the crowd intended to do its part to help their team achieve victory. With every play, the crowd cheered its approval of a hard-hitting football game.

When we lined up to play that night, it was evident that the opposing team was a little bigger than we were and a little faster than we were. By halftime, it became apparent that we were somewhat outmatched. As we walked into our locker room, I remember looking up at the scoreboard and seeing a two-touchdown deficit. There wasn't much talking amongst my teammates as we entered our locker room. We were all feeling the weight of disappointment.

Our head coach began to give us a breakdown of the game, making some adjustments, both on the offensive and defensive sides of the ball. We all took mental notes of the needed changes and waited to be addressed by another coach. My favorite assistant coach stepped up to the lectern to address the team. He was usually very brief and direct in his remarks, but what he said always seemed to have great value. As he approached the team, he simply said these words: "This game will be won by the team who wants to win the most."

As we marched back onto the field for the second half, the stands stood and cheered in our honor. They wanted a win, but could we deliver? The game seemed to be pretty even for most of the third quarter, but we had to do better than just even: We were fourteen points behind. We had an unsuccessful offensive series, and had to punt the ball. Our kicker kicked a high booming punt downfield and their return man caught it and began racing up the field.

With great speed and grace this young athlete moved yard after yard. He was cutting left and right, zigging and zagging all over the field. Our players were diving at him and falling all over the place as they collapsed to the ground in disappointment. As he continued toward the end zone, he was only a few yards away from the score. If he was successful, our team would be down by three touchdowns. This would surely seal our fate. Just at the time when it looked like his success was all but complete, it happened. It was the spark we needed to stay in the game.

One of our players came out of nowhere and hit the ball carrier in the side. He hit him with such force that the ball popped out of his hands and into the hands of one of our players. Our teammate ran in the other direction as fast as he could. It all happened so fast that I don't even think he realized what was going on until he was about midfield! The other team was just as stunned as we were. They thought they had the score. It looked like it was a done deal. Before anyone could gather themselves and respond, our guy crossed the goal line for a touchdown!

Needless to say, the home team stands went berserk. The cheerleaders cheered, the band played at an ear shattering volume, and we celebrated like there was no tomorrow. This one play, this simple mishap by the opposing team, changed the outcome of that game. This single play provided the spark that gave our team the confidence we needed to win that night. That spark generated a momentum shift that hot Florida night that seemed to magically propel us into believing in ourselves again.

The cheering went on for so long that we were actually penalized for delaying the game. We were so happy that we didn't care. We went from a two-touchdown deficit in the third quarter, to winning the game by ten points. This game would be remembered by the fans of that small town for years, and is still one of my "glory days" stories I love to tell my kids.

What happened that memorable Friday night is the magical component that many times leads to the underdog victory. This component is often sought after, but not easily achieved. The spark is that moment when the momentum swings violently in the opposite direction. It swings so hard, in fact, that what seemed to be completely out of reach is now attainable and even probable.

The spark is that moment when the momentum swings violently in the opposite direction.

The story of Ehud is one of the greatest illustrations of this very thing. The people of Israel were discouraged and felt like national victory was completely out of their reach. They had the ability to overcome, but lacked the belief in themselves to pursue it. What they needed was something bigger than they were; they needed something that would restore hope; they needed a reason to believe again: They needed a spark!

> "But Ehud had escaped while they delayed, and passed beyond the stone images and escaped to Seirah. And it happened, when he arrived, that he blew the trumpet in the mountains of Ephraim, and the children of Israel went down with him from the mountains; and he led them. Then he said to them, 'Follow me, for the Lord has delivered your enemies the Moabites into your hand.' So they went down after him, seized the fords of the Jordan leading to Moab, and did not allow anyone to cross over. And at that time they killed about ten thousand men of Moab, all stout men of valor; not a man escaped. So Moab was subdued that day under the hand of Israel. And the land had rest for eighty years" (Judges 3:26-30).

Ehud's assassination of Eglon wasn't the end of the story. On the contrary, his act that day was a declaration of war against the Moabite people. For eighteen years, the Israelites had believed they were inferior and too weak to overtake the people of Moab. They had bought into this lie. It was their reality, and they thought they just had to deal with it. It wasn't until Ehud's obedience provided the needed spark that the people were willing to take up arms and attack their oppressors.

A Simple Spark

What is it that's holding you back? What is the one thing that seems to be holding you down and preventing you from achieving your dreams or fulfilling the calling of your life? You may not need a fully comprehensive game plan that begins now and takes you into the future. What you may need right now is a simple spark. A spark has such potential for power. It can be the catalyst you need to both motivate and empower you to succeed.

I live in the state of Florida, and, like other similar climates, we often have to endure large forest fires during the dry months. During this time it isn't uncommon for us to walk outside and see a haze of smoke from a fire hundreds of miles away. These brushfires can burn for weeks at a time and burn hundreds or even thousands of acres. News crews will show overhead footage from helicopters which reveal flames shooting way into the air. These fires can be costly and even threaten the homes and businesses of local communities. As massive as these fires are though, they all start with a simple spark. Possibly a careless cigarette butt thrown out of a moving car onto the roadside. Maybe a lightning strike onto an old dead tree that immediately goes up in flames. Regardless of the origin, the fire starts with a tiny flame that picks up momentum and eventually turns into a raging forest fire.

What you may need right now is a simple spark.

The spark that we desperately need can come from any number of places. Pain is sometimes a great motivator; as negative as that is, it is sometimes what we need to help us realize that action is in order. Reward is another potential spark; we can be so focused on the reward that we are willing to do whatever it takes to get us to that point. No matter where the spark comes from, it can be the start of an entirely new reality.

As Ehud blew the trumpet in the mountains of Ephraim, it was the sound of war. This was the rallying cry to get the troops to assemble. This was not a general informational summit; it was a call for war against the evil Moabites. When the men heard this trumpet blast they knew what it meant. Each man grabbed his sword and convened to hear the battle plan.

What happened that day was nothing short of a miracle. This was no small battle between two little cities that had a disagreement. This was all-out war between two nations. One nation was a powerful and evil oppressor, and the other nation was tired of being subservient and had had enough. This was an epic battle that was eighteen years in the making. Take note that this battle had little demonstrated preparation.

When Ehud called the people to the mountains of Ephraim, it was to make ready for war. He didn't start a boot camp, or begin to go over training techniques to prepare his people for war. As the people gathered, there was no sword sharpening or bow stringing. When the men showed, it was expected that they were ready to go to war immediately. The men, who responded to the sound of the trumpet were men who were already ready to fight and overcome the Moabites. Ehud offered them nothing that day to make them better warriors; he simply told them the story of a king he had assassinated.

These men were already strong enough and significantly trained enough to go to war and succeed. This battle could have taken place years earlier, and potentially had the same results. Ehud didn't offer a specific guaranteed training regimen, but he was bold enough to ask the hard question. "Men, are you ready to experience freedom for the first time in eighteen years?"

My point here is simple: These men already had the ability to overcome the Moabites within them. Ehud's actions did not strengthen the military might of this assembly, but they did cause them to believe in themselves once again. The left-handed warrior was no magician or even a military genius, but he did offer what these people had been lacking for eighteen years: a spark.

They had already been motivated to go to war all these years. They had lived in the pain of being a subservient nation, the pain of knowing their children were always under the watchful eye of an oppressive entity, and the economic pain that a large portion of their nation's goods were always committed to the evil leader of Moab. These reasons were motivation to consider war, but they weren't enough to motivate them to actually pursue war.

As pain was a motivator, so was reward. I'm sure the people of Israel dreamt of what it would be like to be a sovereign nation again. The reward of a military victory would last for generations and restore hope for a secure and vibrant future once again. Without a doubt, a powerful motivator could be found in the reward of victory. Yet with all the potential motivation available and with all the military power that was present, they were still missing that one ingredient that could change their future.

This ingredient, of course, was their own belief in themselves as children of God. This belief wouldn't come easy, it wouldn't be cheap; it would take more than a pep talk or an inspirational quote. For this belief in themselves to begin to take shape and build upon itself and lead to freedom, there would have to be a spark.

God Has Chosen You!

This book isn't written for the purpose of a history lesson about the nation of Israel. This book is written to hopefully provide the needed spark to get you to believe in yourself and God's plan for your life once again. We know that God can do the impossible. We know that God is all-powerful, and that He is almighty. However, do you realize that He chooses to use people *like us* to reveal His power and might?

Do you realize that He chooses to use people *like us* to reveal His power and might?

> "Now to Him who is able to do exceedingly abundantly above all that we ask or think, according to the power that works in us" (Ephesians 3:20).

Paul says, that God is able to do *exceedingly and abundantly* above all that we ask or even think! *Exceedingly and abundantly!* These words are seldom ever used like this in the same sentence. He is making a point here: We serve a God without limitations. He says, "above all that we ask or think." I don't know about you, but I can think of some pretty big things. God says His abilities far surpass even that. Now here's the real kicker: He says, "according to the power that works in us." How is all of this revealed in the earth? How are all of these exceeding and abundant things made manifest? They happen as a result of the power that works in us.

God doesn't use us out of some sort of self-imposed obligation. He uses us because He delights in seeing His creation fulfilling the purpose for which they were created. Nothing brings greater joy to a father than seeing his children living up to their potential and growing in their gifts and abilities.

> "For by Him all things were created that are in heaven and that are on earth, visible and invisible, whether thrones or dominions or principalities or powers. All things were created through Him and for Him" (Colossians 1:16).

There is a power that works inside of us to bring forth the plans that God intended for the earth. We were created to do wonderful things. Doing incredible things isn't just an option, like an ice cream flavor at a local sweet shop; it was what we were born to do. Never doubt that God intended you for greatness. Even if you've made some mistakes along the way, He wants to see you succeed!

Believe in Yourself

Ehud had to believe in himself before he could ever inspire an army of warriors. What got them on his side? Was it simply the news that he had killed the king? I don't think so. If anything, this could have backfired and caused them to retreat in terror. I believe they saw a self-determination in his faith that was absolutely contagious. They couldn't help but be inspired by him. They didn't simply agree to take up arms and go to war, they wholeheartedly embraced the opportunity with enthusiasm and vigor. There was a spark of faith in Ehud that lit the crowd with a burning faith that could only be satisfied by defeating their enemies.

Ehud had to believe in himself before he could ever inspire an army of warriors.

When the cries of the oppressed Israelites reached the ears of God, He knew He had to get His message to them. He had to get them to once again believe that they were the powerful people who He had ordained them to be. He had to get them to remember that they were a chosen nation with a rich history of victory against all odds. He wanted them to know that they had usually been the underdogs for much of their history, but that really didn't matter. God wanted them to believe in Him once again, and He wanted them to believe in themselves for the first time in over eighteen years.

This message sent by God did not come in any normal fashion. This message was different from most any story the people had ever heard before. In fact, this message was delivered in such a way that it would go down in history as one of the greatest upsets of all time. This message took the form of a left-handed warrior, a man who was willing to stand against all odds and risk his life to assassinate the king who had held them captive for years on end. The message of revitalizing the faith of the people began with a spark and then quickly developed into a raging forest fire of victory.

Maybe you are searching for your spark. You might be looking for that one thing to get you motivated to take on that big obstacle or insurmountable task. Look no further than the person in the mirror. As the Israelites possessed the power to defeat the Moabites well before Ehud killed the king, you also have what you need to be successful. Your success is not built on a feeling: Most people feel inadequate when they first begin to pursue extreme challenges. Your success must come from the realization that the Lord has prepared you for anything you will ever encounter.

Your success must come from the realization that the Lord has prepared you for anything you will ever encounter.

I'm sure Ehud's assignment looked impossible when he first began to consider actually following through with it. The people of Israel were oppressed by feelings of inferiority when they thought of attacking Moab; we know that because it took them eighteen years to do it. Never let the size of the task undermine the depth of your faith. Allow your faith to go before your task, with full confidence in the Lord that He will never let you down, and know that He is with you every step of the way.

There is a seesaw mentality among followers of Christ today. One moment people are up on cloud nine and the very next they are so discouraged they can hardly mutter a prayer. Serving Jesus shouldn't be based on an emotionally-driven experience, constantly contingent on how we perceive the progress of our lives. Truthfully, when you're serving Jesus, there will be some difficult days. However, when you are not serving Jesus, there will also be some pretty difficult days.

Never let the size of the task undermine the depth of your faith.

Do you think it was easy or difficult for Ehud to consider, decide upon, and implement his assassination attempt? It was difficult! It was the hardest thing he ever did during his entire life. Was it difficult? Yes! Nevertheless, was it rewarding? You had better believe it! Never base your decision about whether or not to take on an obstacle solely on its level of difficulty. You serve a God who is able to take the most impossible task and turn it into a reality.

The same God who took a left-handed nobody and turned him into a national hero and inspiration for generations to come is the same God who is working on your behalf. Don't believe that that difficult promotion is out of reach for you. Don't buy into the notion that you don't deserve God's very best for your life. Don't believe for a second that God will have to use someone else to do the big things because you're not able. Don't fall into the trap of allowing your own self-doubt to keep you from being a left-handed warrior.

After Ehud's rally cry and trumpet sound in the hills of Ephraim, the Israelites went on to kill about ten thousand Moabite men. This wasn't just a small battle; this wasn't a few kids having a backyard baseball showdown. This was a major war and a major victory for the people of Israel. This didn't just mean they could celebrate for a few moments either. It meant generations would be blessed as a result of their faithfulness. The spark that Ehud lit was a game changer in the fullest sense of the word.

This victory would secure peace over all the land of Israel. Now God's chosen people were no longer under the strong and wicked iron fist of Eglon or any other king for that matter. They lived in God's peace and prosperity for a full eighty years, one of the longest stints of peace in their entire history. All of this occurred because of a little spark by the name of Ehud.

I want to challenge you: Be that spark! Believe in what God can do through you as Ehud did! Believe in yourself, even when it seems as if nobody else does. Dare to believe God for the impossible. Never let the Enemy undermine your value. It's time to dream once again. It's time to believe like never before. You are the one nobody ever saw coming. It's time to cue up the band and let the left-handed warriors arise.

About the Author

Jamie Jones is the lead pastor at Trinity Church in Deltona, Florida. Under his leadership, the church has seen tremendous growth and expansion. Pastor Jamie also oversees a network of pastors and churches in western Honduras and travels preaching and teaching church leadership and revival. Over the years, he and his wife, Michelle, of over twenty-five years, along with their three children, Kristen, James, and Joshua, have been involved in church planting, missions, evangelism, and local outreach. His message is one of hope, restoration, and a true desire for spiritual awakening.

Jamie can be contacted at revjpjones@yahoo.com.

We are a Christian-based publishing company that was founded in 2009. Our primary focus has been to establish authors.

"5 Fold Media was the launching partner that I needed to bring *The Transformed Life* into reality. This team worked diligently and with integrity to help me bring my words and vision into manifestation through a book that I am proud of and continues to help people and churches around the world. None of this would have been possible without the partnership and education I received from 5 Fold Media."

- Pastor John Carter, Lead Pastor of Abundant Life Christian Center, Syracuse, NY, Author and Fox News Contributor

**The Transformed Life* is foreworded by Pastor A.R. Bernard, received endorsements from best-selling authors Phil Cooke, Rick Renner, and Tony Cooke, and has been featured on television shows such as TBN and local networks

5 Fold Media
5701 E. Circle Dr. #338, Cicero, NY 13039
manuscript@5foldmedia.com

Find us on Facebook, Twitter, and YouTube

Discover more at www.5FoldMedia.com.